Becoming a Web Designer…

Becoming a Web Designer...

Skilled in the Ancient Art of Llama Herding

Aaron Wester

Writers Club Press

San Jose New York Lincoln Shanghai

Becoming a Web Designer...
Skilled in the Ancient Art of Llama Herding

Writers Club Press
an imprint of iUniverse, Inc.

For information address:
iUniverse, Inc.
5220 S. 16th St., Suite 200
Lincoln, NE 68512
www.iuniverse.com

ISBN: 0-595-21591-2

Printed in the United States of America

I would like to dedicate this book to my wonderful and brilliant wife Jeannette. Without her efforts and patience, this book would not be.

CONTENTS

ACKNOWLEDGEMENTS

I would like to thank all the hard working Llama herders for their unwavering dedication to the professional field of manual labor. Without them, the streets would be utter chaos rampaged by the tyranny of Llamas all over the world.

In fact, it's Llama herders like Diane, Doug, Gary, Brian, Leroy, Brad, Marylynn, Ellis, Beverly, Sean, Jim, and Pat that keep us all safe from this terrible threat to society!

1. Welcome

1.1 Welcome to the Wonderful World of Web (WWW)

Congratulations on your new guide to success. Of course, I'm referring to the guide in which you are currently reading.

You are probably thinking to yourself, 'well, I'm sure on my way to riches now. After all, I've just purchased this all-encompassing guide that's sure to change my life for the better. Now I'll just go outside and pick weeds with my bare hands, because purchasing the guide and actually reading it are two entirely different things all together.'

With this in mind, it's important that I offer you a brief introduction that convinces you of the necessity for reading, evaluating, studying, and applying the applications in this guide to ensure your ultimate success. After all, it's a win/win situation for both of us. I've written a comprehensive book that will teach you the skills necessary to landing the greatest job in the world. In return, you'll learn the skills most necessary in making millions of dollars in the Internet industry. This of course will cause you to send unsolicited gratuitous donations to help me purchase several new Ferrari's for all my friends.

Chances are, you are one of millions of people that have recently discovered how impacting the Internet has become to our economic prosperity. If you are like me, then you too have fallen into one of the following situations, thus leading you to take immediate action, such as moving to Guam to raise Chihuahua herds.

Situation 1: You went to the local mini mart for milk. However, instead of being greeted by the welcoming neon sign stating 'Open 24 Hours', you were greeted instead by a boarded up front door, gated and locked with the following sign nailed to it. "Have taken the business Dot Com. Please visit our new web site for your milk and grocery needs..."

Situation 2: You were offered a job working for pennies in a garage with a couple of longhaired, pocket protector friends to help them launch a new web site. You called them geeks, pointed and laughed at them, then went to your not so cozy 9 to 5 job. A couple months later you received a phone call from your friends. Their little garage web site had been purchased for 100 billion dollars, and they just wanted to tell you about how happy they were with retirement on their newly purchased island, Hawaii (coincidentally, they had to go because lobsters were being served on the veranda with margaritas).

Although these are only extreme examples that represent the reality of the high tech Internet movement, the simple fact of the matter is clear. It's time to move to Guam to raise Chihuahuas. NO! Actually, it's time to take an impacting step forward in the evolutionary process, and read, evaluate, study and most importantly, apply the applications in this guide so you too can reap from the benefits of the Internet Industry. Welcome to the Wonderful World of Web (WWW).

1.2 WWW (The World Wide Web)

What exactly is the World Wide Web? Chances are fairly good that you've seen a commercial recently advertising something www or other. For instance, some of the most expensive commercials dueling for your attention during the 1999 Super Bowl Sunday were WWW in nature. They were companies that competed in a web market environment, and in most cases were companies that only exist on an e-business platform, that is to say, a Dot Com company.

It's historically well known that the Internet was created by the United States Government for military tactical purposes. For instance, I am a firm believer that the best minds in the military set out with billions of our tax dollars to create the ultimate multi player network for Solitaire (Codename: Internet), until they discovered that Solitaire was a single player game. Livid with the idea that Solitaire couldn't be played with others, they scrapped the project, and sold the Internet to a pimply eight year-old boy in Delaware for $15.00 plus his Star Wars collection (including Star Wars Monopoly, which is a multi player game!). That would ultimately explain why years later, the Internet is still run by a pimply sixteen year old boy in Delaware off his hard drive.

Although none of this is factually accurate, it is however what I firmly believe. I don't want you to take my word for it though, therefor I will include a more accurate rendition of the World Wide Web for your personal enjoyment.

The Internet (net for short), is literally a network of computers that are all connected together around the world. The World Wide Web, or WWW for short was created by Tim Berner-Lees as an internet-based hypermedia initiative for global information sharing. Tim created the first GUI (Graphical User Interface) based web browser and is the literal founder of the web (He still however drives a thirteen year old Volkswagon Rabbit). Most major web sites are found using this initiative (for a more detailed history of the World Wide Web, please visit the following location on the internet: *http://www.w3.org/History.html*). For instance, *www.yahoo.com* (a web portal that lets you search for literally anything on the Internet. And I really mean anything. For instance, my wife had me look up 'park bench' once on yahoo. It spit out tons of results ranging from rock bands named Park Bench, to park bench manufacturers, to organizations who's sole purpose is to save park benches from extinction. Who would've thought.), *ebay.com* (only the largest auction site community in the entire universe.

And this is taking into account Bill's Bingo and Auction House just north of Nowhereville.), and *buy.com* (an extremely large online retailer that competes for my business every day and considers me a valued customer. At least that's what their email says.) all have unique addresses on the net that can be viewed using a web browser, and can be found on the World Wide Web. Coincidentally, these three web sites started out originally as pre-IPO Dot Com companies, tailoring only to customers that browsed the web. All three of these companies are now publicly traded on the NASDAQ, and have made many web designers extremely rich. Many of them are currently retired and now own Europe, but that's a different story all together.

1.3 Who REALLY is the Dot in Dot Com and what's a pre-IPO?

A while ago, Sun Microsystems launched a very aggressive marketing campaign to convince the world that they were truly the Dot in Dot Com. However, it came to their attention that no one really knew what the heck that meant, so Sun quietly dropped the campaign from the main stream. To this day you may still see tattered and torn, worn out posters with this slogan, which you could probably sell on ebay for hundreds of thousands of dollars. Most people however will more than likely want a refund when they read the slogan and wonder what the heck it meant.

So obviously, you are now asking yourself, 'who really IS the Dot in Dot Com', and more importantly 'when do we get to the part about me making millions of dollars?'.

Fortunately, you're now in possession of a guide who's goal is to help you discern between the Dots and the Dots in Dot Coms, whatever that means.

A basic 'Dot Com' company such as *www.billsbingoandauctionhouse.com*, isn't going to get you very far as a web designer when your goal is to make millions. Let's put this company into a quick 'Dot in Dot Com' evaluation, to see if they have what it takes to make it big.

1. Their web name is WAY too long, and hard to remember.

2. They think a General Counselor is spelled 'lauyerr', and believe their only purpose is to post bail when necessary.

3. Their funding comes from Bill's sixteen years of life savings, amounting to a few hundred dollars, but is added to liquid assets such as his dentures, and lifelong collection of newspapers.

4. They're located in the sunny, bustling, downtown, metropolitan area of Russia, Ohio.

5. They claim they're a transnational company because they are strategically located in Russia, Ohio.

6. They think Seed Funding is for farming.

This is opposed to the 'Dot in Dot Com' kind of company that offers unique services to customers, businesses and Llama's alike such as *www.ebay.com*. Before ebay went public, they had a lot of market potential. The goal of ebay was to create a one on one environment for trading goods in an auction based format. This was a concept that was new to the Internet back in 1995. Let's take a moment to stress test ebay against our 'Dot in Dot Com' evaluation.

1. Their web name is catchy, and easy to remember.

2. They hired a strong staff that would carry them through the long haul of going from pre-IPO to publicly traded on the NASDAQ.

3. They received the necessary funding to cover expenses until they could turn a profit.

4. They're located in sunny San Jose, California. Which is where many other successful Internet companies boast from.

5. They are a transnational company, trading in foreign territories and States all over the world.

6. They know that Seed Funding can make a farmer very rich! (Seed Funding is given to startup companies by Venture Capital Firms

looking to back a solid business idea. The funding can range any-where from a few hundred dollars to millions and millions of dollars)

So in answer to the question, 'Who REALLY is the Dot in Dot Com?', I would most certainly have to answer that it is dependent on several factors, including who they are, what they do, where their financing comes from, what is their niche, what is their potential, where are they located, and most importantly, are they willing to send me gratuitous donations. Although there are several other factors involved, I only want to introduce you to a few major ones first.

If you still haven't gathered what all this hoopla is about concerning pre-IPO's, then let me take a quick moment to bring you into the now. The major pushing force for any startup Dot Com company is swift and quick success as a publicly traded company on the stock market. This is where the strongest incentive is for web designers who yearn to make a quick million bucks.

A pre-IPO company is simply a company that has yet to introduce an Initial Public Offering on the stock market. However, there are many obstacles that stand in the way of a company before it can reach the IPO stage, and even then, the company risks not being well received by speculative investors. The company could go under at any given stage of the process if they haven't lived up to the 'Dot in Dot Com' evaluation. For instance, the company could run out of funding before filing with the SEC (United States Securities Exchange Commission). The SEC might deny the company from going public due to application mishandling, or because the company hurt the SEC's feelings by calling them bad names when the SEC denied the paperwork.

It can be safely assumed that working for a pre-IPO Dot Com company might not be for the faint of heart. However, your chances at scoring big on just the right startup Internet company with minimal risk can be obtained simply by following the easy outlined steps in this guide. I have taken great pains (heartburn from late night pizza while tirelessly writing this book, that is...), in ensuring that this guide covers all the major stepping stones in choosing just the right company to work for. As well as how to even get the job as a well experienced web designer. That's right! You too can become a seasoned veteran, who like many of us, will end up in a rocking chair at age eighty nagging your great grand children about how when you were younger, you had to develop web sites in snow storms, up hill both ways.

2. Building Your First Web Home

2.1 Finding Land to Build On

In order for anyone to become a successful web designer, they must first know the very basics of developing for the web. However, if you feel that you're already a web designer guru, and have an incredibly strong understanding of how a web site is constructed, then you might want to consider fast forwarding to Chapter 3. I would still argue that you should definitely read this chapter so that you don't hurt my feelings, But most importantly because I'll cover extremely complex algorithms that explicitly detail the process for having total strangers just throw money at you where ever you go. Actually, I have no intention whatsoever in sharing these complex algorithms with you. Mainly I just don't want you to hurt my feelings. We will however be covering important information concerning site functionality, performance, and layout.

I'm going to spend this chapter detailing the process of creating a web site from scratch. In fact, we're going to develop an entire virtual mansion. (I was originally going to have you develop a virtual mobile home, but it just wasn't the same…)

Creating a web site is very much like constructing a home. Actually, come to think of it, I've never really built a home before, nor do I have the slightest clue how one is built. I did build a snap together model airplane once though, so I imagine it can't be much more difficult than that.

Now then, when looking for a place to build, you must decide on several important features that can have a direct impact on the reliability and speed to accessing the web site. Your web site won't do people much good if they can't connect to it due to performance issues. There are steps you can initially take though, that will lessen the chances for poor performance. The first of these is...

2.1.1 Choosing an Internet Account

There are several different kinds of Internet Services that are provided for aspiring web designers. In fact, chances are that you're currently connecting to the internet through an ISP (Internet Service Provider, such as Earthlink and AT&T WorldNet) or Network Provider (such as AOL and Prodigy) that offers you a free amount of web space to build with. The best way to check on this, is to contact a generous representative for your ISP or Network Provider. Tell them that you would like to start a trust fund in their name with millions of dollars in it, and have a pencil & paper ready as they excitedly tell you all about your free web site account, and how to access it.

Actually, I've worked for several ISPs in the past, so I can tell you from experience that this probably won't get you very far. They will however happily put you on hold for several minutes, until you've hung up so they can kindly thank the dial tone and be on their way to lunch. In fact, one of the Customer Service jokes for most major ISPs is 'Please hold for the dial tone'. There are ways around this though. When you get a representative on the phone, tell them you have questions about the services that come with your account. Chances are that they will refer you to the proper person for further information, or to a web page they maintain that contains detailed instructions on receiving your free web space. If they are in a bad mood however, they may instead simply transfer you to the queue for the shipping department where you will wait for 45 minutes, until someone feels like picking up the phone, who will then gladly transfer you to sales where you will be greeted immediately, and then placed on hold for 45 minutes. This isn't really a bad thing though, because at least in sales, they will throw you a sales pitch on purchasing a web site space. This would then give you a terrific chance in getting answers such as...

2.1.2 What's the Difference between a Free vs. Paid Web Site Account?

One of the biggest differences between free web site and paid web site accounts is that sales agents don't get a commission for selling you a free web site. With that in mind, let's go over some major details between the two choices.

Free web sites are generally given out as a gratuity for paying a monthly service charge for Internet access. You'll notice for instance, that although some ISP's offer free Internet access, they don't necessarily offer a free web site space. An example of this would be Netzero (*http://www.netzero.net*), who offers outstanding access to the internet for free, in exchange for running advertisements across your desktop while you're connected to the Internet. They give each free account an email address, but not a free web site space. If you fall into this category of users, then you should consider something similar to Homestead (*http://www.homestead.com*), which is a service on the Internet that provides free web sites to every registered account holder. Earthlink (*http://www.earthlink.net*), another ISP, offers access to the internet for a monthly charge, and with their accounts come email and a 6mb free web site space. 6mb is another way of saying 6 megabytes of space. However, if you're anything at all like me, then you are probably looking at the term '6mb', and wondering whether that's like 6ft or 6cm, so let me explain. Considering that a single character such as the letter 'a' takes about 3 bytes of space, then use the following chart to see how large a 6mb web site space really is.

Letter 'a' = 3 bytes
1,024 bytes = 1 kilobyte
1,024 kilobytes = 1 megabyte
6 megabytes = 1 free Earthlink web site space

In other words, you can type millions of the letter 'a' and still have plenty of room for the letter 'b'! In all seriousness though, it's not the letters that usually take all the space. Any images you use on your web site will take considerable space as well. We will be covering this more in section 2.4.1, 'Building within size constraints'.

Free web sites make excellent starter sites for the newbie designer as they provide a safe testing ground for creating neat mistakes that cannot be fixed without the aid of a few matches and some gasoline. This is because one of the most terrible downsides to free web spaces is lack of support from professional technical type people. If your web site goes off line and you need help fixing it, your chances for web support are slim to none. Some companies do offer email support though, which means that if you ever got hold of their phone number, to actually speak to a human being, they would immediately disconnect all the phones, change their company name, and move to Canada. Coincidentally, this would explain why so many Internet companies are based in Canada.

Paid web sites on the other hand are at the other end of the spectrum. First and foremost, they cost more. When you purchase a web site account, you aren't actually buying a tangible object. You are in many ways, simply leasing a storage space on somebody else's computer network. There are advantages and disadvantages to choosing this path.

On the plus side, your web site would have much more space to work with. Generally, a paid web site starts at 10mb (feel free to use 10ft or 10cm if this helps at all...). Also, if you need additional space later, your sales agent will be more than happy to sell you the super deluxe, turbo charged, quasi, sub woofer based site upgrade with a lifetime guarantee or no money back!

You can generally get better technical web support as well. In fact, more often than not, a paid site entitles you to a web support hotline phone number, and a gold plated key to their restrooms. The site will also generally tend to load faster on the web browser than free web sites (more on this in the next section).

On the downside though, paid web sites take longer to setup initially by whichever company will by hosting it. This is because more work is involved in setting up your paid web site on their end, than a free web site. Also, you aren't just charged for the web site. You are also charged for the web site address, which we will cover in this chapter, as well as traffic. The traffic is defined as the users that visit your web site. If you have a very popular web site, you might have to pay a toll charge at some point for having an excessive amount of traffic. I know you're thinking, 'can't I just setup an online toll booth to collect money from the users that rack up all the charges?!', and my answer would have to be, 'nice try, but no.'.

2.1.3 Connection speeds

Free web sites are much slower than paid web sites. Generally when someone is paying money for a web site space, they tend to expect a fast loading page, on their web browser. There are many reasons why a web site will load slowly, including poorly scripted programming, graphic images that take to long to load, and Internet congestion. However, the most basic reason is that the site is crammed onto a server (the storage space where your web site resides) that already hosts more web sites than it can handle. In a very real sense, this creates bottleneck, where the server must handle too many processes, thus taking decades to load a single page of code on a web site.

Most free web site spaces are handled in this fashion. This is because servers are expensive, and since you aren't paying anything for the darned site anyway, why should they shell out more dollars for another web server?!

Paid web sites on the other hand, are generally much faster for just the opposite reason. The Service Provider that hosts your site, realizes that you can go elsewhere to have your site hosted if they aren't up to par with the speed required in serving up your site. Therefor, great pains are usually taken to keep a minimum number of sites on a single server.

If you're wondering how long a site should normally take to load, my general rule of thumb is to hold your breath. If the site still hasn't fully loaded by the time you've passed out, then chances are it's loading too slowly. Actually, it should really only take between 30 to 60 seconds to load.

You must remember though that there are other factors involved that could be slowing down the transfer of information. For instance, a poor Internet connection can cause line noise that can corrupt your online session, and web sites that are heavily graphics oriented, can take awhile to load as well. Plus if you find that the web site tends to only load slowly at peak hours of the day, such as 12pm and 6pm, then this is usually because of net congestion, which is much like Los Angeles rush hour traffic. In this case though, instead of staring mindlessly at some parked Ford Pento's bumper in the fast lane for hours on end, you get to relish the opportunity of staring at your blank monitor well into the morning. Net congestion is usually caused by your phone line being backed up with traffic of users, most of whom are frequently engaged in the thrilling hobby of staring blankly at their monitors after spending several hours in rush hour traffic.

2.1.4 The client/server relationship

The Internet is a pretty amazing gizmo if you stop and think about it. All those computers connected together, forming an amazingly complex and sophisticated network of terminals all having access to pages and pages of information! It reminds me of a similar project I created in my computer class back when I was attending junior high school. My teacher gave it a miserable failing grade, but it still accomplished essentially what the Internet is designed to do. Basically, I programmed a page that had a single sentence reading 'Click here for more'. Then it would direct you to a new page with a lone sentence that read 'Click here for more'. This exciting process went on and on, into an infinite loop, giving my classmates instant gratification as we watched our teacher throw a massive fit of rage in a pointless attempt at exiting the program. Although I feel fully justified in taking ample credit for creating the worlds first Internet, let's take a brief look at what makes the real Internet work.

We now know that the Internet is a global network of computers all connected together, but it's now time to get a little more technical. The computer that you work on from the comforts of your home, or work, or at play, or whatever, is basically a 'client terminal'. We learned earlier that a server is basically the storage space where your web site resides. More in-depth, a server can be either a 'stand alone', or a 'client resident program' that performs certain applications on a client terminal. Now you are thinking, 'huh?!'.

A stand-alone server can be extremely expensive ranging from a few thousand dollars to a few hundred thousand dollars. This is because a stand-alone server is meant to serve, as its literary name foretells. These devices come in large tower cases that can be mounted to a rack full of other servers. They usually offer multiple hard drives, and have several cooling fans on the processors. These devices are extremely storage capable, and add that extra touch of Star Trek flavor to any home deco.

Client resident programs are run directly from your computer (alias: client terminal). Some servers don't serve as a primary storage means, therefore making it unnecessary to serve at a larger capacity. For instance, if you wanted to host a full time chat room that was always open to the general public, you could easily run a chat server from your local client terminal, and never have to purchase a stand-alone server.

The Internet is made possible in part, due to the client/server relationship, or in other words, the connection that your home computer makes to the server that is handled on the other end of the telephone line. Just thank your lucky stars that these relationships aren't any closer than they already are. You'd start with a hot client/server relationship, and before you know it, you'd be raising cute little laptops. Remember to practice safe client/server relationships whenever possible.

2.1.5 What's a domain name, and who the heck is URL?

Why Dot Com, when you can just as easily Dot Gov or Dot Org, or Dot Net?! The answer lies in what a web address really is, how it is read as a URL, and how it is translated into a true IP address. Of course, if you send your CD via DVD with your VCR, ASAP, this might all make a little more sense, so let me explain in greater detail.

When you have a free web site, you share the same virtual name with hundreds of other people. The only difference is that you would need to add your username directly after the web address, to specifically choose your site from the bucket of others. On Earthlink for instance, every free web site user first types in *http://home.earthlink.net* to get to their site, but in order to complete this request, they must also add /~username to the end of the address. So it now looks like *http://home.earthlink.net/~bub-basmochafactory*.

This doesn't look as professional though if you are running an expensive high tech company from the Internet. This is where paid web sites become useful. One of the reasons that paid web sites take sooooo long in setting up is because the ISP must map a unique 'domain name' to your new web site location on their servers. The domain name is unique in that you can only use the name once at a time on the Internet. So if someone beats you to the punch on the bright sounding web site *www.Milk4U2!.com*, you can forget using that name either until their lease on the name is up, or until you negotiate the purchase of their lease.

Domain names are leased to the general public. No one actually owns the name. When you first select a name, you are given a two-year lease with an option to update the lease each year thereafter. The initial two year lease costs under $100 to initiate, and then usually under $50 each year thereafter to maintain. These costs are usually added to your bill when you pay for your web site. The company you choose to cohost your web site will usually make all the necessary arrangements with securing a domain name for you.

A domain name is categorized into different specialties. For instance, if you are starting a business for a network of frogs, you might consider using the domain name *www.frogs.net*. Notice the extension, .net? This is one of several distinct extensions used to categorize web specialties. The main list breaks down as follows:

.com—For commerce sites such as retail, businesses and entertainment. Most commonly used on the net.

.net—For networks that wish to offer services ranging from hosting to general.

Sometimes used as an alternative to the .com extension.

.gov—Government agencies get dibs on this extension.

.org—Non-profit organizations, and charity sites flock to this high vegetation platform.

Also, there are several country domain name extensions (such as .uk, .sg, .de) but unless you plan on developing a web site in a more foreign language than English, then it's best that you stay away from unique country domains. There are reasons for extending your site to a wider international clientele, but we will cover this more fully later in the book.

Domain names were part of a United States Federal Government plan, with the help of the InterNIC, to encourage the privatization and commercialization of the Internet. They are now issued by companies such as Network Solutions (*http://www.networksolutions.com*), otherwise known by their slogan as the 'The Dot Com People'. They are the leading registrar of domain names on the Internet, and coincidentally a publicly traded company on the NASDAQ.

So what's in a name, you ask? Well, all I can suggest is that you ask URL. U.R.L stands for Uncontrollable Rabid Llama, but more importantly it stands for Uniform Resource Locator. Since you are viewing a file maintained on another computer when visiting a specific web address, the URL is what makes it possible for you to find a file across a network. Essentially, if you leased a paid web site, and had chosen the domain name *http://www.bubbasmochafactory.com*, then this would serve as your URL as well. The reason for this is that when you visit the web site, you will be taken by server default to the main 'home page' of the web site, which might serve as the starting point of several pages that make up an entire web site. The 'home page' is a file with a unique filename, possibly called index.htm or index.html.

These file extensions (.htm, and .html) are very similar to file extensions you might be more familiar with, such as a Microsoft Word document file with the .doc extension. The main difference is that while a word processor such as Microsoft Word looks for the extension .doc when opening a document, the web browser such as Netscape Communicator, or Microsoft Internet Explorer generally search for the extension .htm or .html when loading a web site page. Also, the home page is generally called index because the server can only default to a specific name, and index is as good a name as any.

Finally, take the easy to remember domain name *www.ThereReallyIsn'taWebSiteByThisName.com* for example. Imagine however, how much more difficult it would be if instead, you had to remember 432.231.121.123.... This series of octets is an IP address, or Internet Protocol Address. Remember how I mentioned earlier that paid web sites took longer to setup because they had to be mapped to the IP address? The domain name has to be mapped to the IP address, because your computer has no clue what *www.WhoopieLand!.com* really means. It only knows that a user typed a request to go to a text location that is currently mapped to go to an IP address such as 207.102.221.154 that it can understand.

There is an alternative method to building your web site. You don't actually need an Internet account of any kind to build a web site, and view it's contents. Instead, you simply build the web site in code, slap on some images, and open your browser to view the site. Because the files that make up your new site reside on your local system's hard drive, the browser can be guided to open those files where ever they may reside. This is a fast and simple way to practice web development, without the weight and burden of setting up a free or paid web site account. The main drawback to this method though, is that you can't expect others to see your work unless you've found another way to get your files and images to their system's hard drive as well.

2.2 Web Tools to Build With

Now that we've taken a moment to figure out where we're actually going to build our new home, let's decide on which tools are most appropriate for the construction phase of the project. Although there are lots of different types of nails and hammers on the market, my intent is not to cover every type available to you. In other words, my main goal in this section is to assure you that when building a web site, hammers and nails do indeed exist regardless of the fact that there are thousands of variations on the basic model. For instance, why have a plain old hammer when you can have a Leather Strapped Titanium based, graphite encased, stainless steel, rot iron hammer with gold leaf melted over the molecular grooves of the surface…My point is, it's STILL a hammer! In the Internet industry you'll find many variations on an original theme, therefore I will cover one or two variances just to give you an idea of what's available and considered useful in the market by top web gurus.

2.2.1 Introduction to the Browsers

Two of the most technologically revolutionizing products that have ever been invented are 1) the Internet browser, and 2) Twinkies. Having had experienced both miraculous products, I'd have to say that my life wouldn't be complete without either of these two items. For instance, without the Internet browser, I couldn't view the contents of a web page. Without Twinkies though, I simply wouldn't have the energy to wait for a web page to load in the browser! So you see, they go hand in hand...

Although I am a certified professional in the field of eating Twinkies, I've come to the conclusion that I'm not the only certified Twinkie Engineer who appreciates their finer value. Therefore we shall instead discuss the other revolutionary product, which is to say Ding Dongs. No, that's not right, what I really mean is the Internet browser.

There are several Internet browsers available on the net. Most of these are freely distributed, which means that you can make a copy of the program for free and run it on your computer. The two major competitors in the market that we'll look more closely at are Microsoft Internet Explorer, and Netscape Communicator. Chances are very good that you are currently running a copy of one of these applications on your computer now, if not both. You might be thinking to yourself, 'That guy's got it all wrong! I use the AOL browser!'...The truth of the matter is that AOL doesn't have it's own browser at all anymore. A couple years back, AOL purchased Netscape for a couple of dollars in change, but AOL also has an arrangement with Microsoft to distribute the Microsoft Internet Explorer browser as well. AOL defaults to Microsoft Internet Explorer, unless you prefer to use Netscape Communicator in which case they are more than happy to accommodate you. You may find slight variations between the browsers offered from competing ISP's and Network Providers, but they still essentially come down to either of these two popular name brands on the Internet.

While we're on the subject of America Online (AOL), AOL isn't really a direct connection to the internet, instead they offer filtered internet connectivity through their extended network of services, therefor they get labeled under canned produce, which is to say Network Providers…This is NOT a bad thing though! An ISP usually focuses on the fastest possible connection to the Internet by reducing the number of extended services to the user. AOL and other Network Providers though take a different approach. They focus on a well-rounded connection to various services, while offering standard connectivity to the WWW (World Wide Web). The ISP's argue that their connections are faster to the WWW because they are bypassing the network services and focusing on a straight shot connection to the Internet. The Network Providers counter this argument with the concept that most users don't want to bother with the conflicting dumpster of media that the Internet offers. They instead offer exclusive services that provide the users with an alternative to seeking for the same information elsewhere, such as chatting, news, weather, sports, etc…In the end, there is no viable solution to this bitter and ongoing feud between the masses of ISP's and Network Providers other than giving water balloons to the employees of each respective competitor, then letting them duke it out. This would make for a very entertaining stadium sport.

Not everyone has the opportunity of using browsers that can handle images. Therefor, it's important that I bring Lynx to your attention. Lynx is a text-only browser that can be obtained as freeware (meaning that it's freely distributed on the Internet). Lynx is a great testing tool as well, because it's a general application browser, which means that generally it's safe to assume that if a web site works well in Lynx, then it will reasonably be usable by people with visual, cognitive, speech, and auditory disabilities.

If you are interested in obtaining Microsoft Internet Explorer, then visit *http://www.microsoft.com*. If you are interested in having a copy of Netscape Communicator, visit *http://www.netscape.com*. If you would like to download Lynx, then visit *http://www.download.com*, and conduct a search for 'Lynx'. You will find the latest version, Lynx 2.8.1

available for download. It's usually a GREAT idea as a web designer to have copies of many different browsers, for testing. Although a web site should by theory load equally on all browsers, there are compatibility issues that we will discuss later, that can greatly impact the overall design and functionality of a web site.

2.2.2 What is HTML and Why Should I Care?

I shouldn't have to say I told you so, but you knew it was coming. The dreaded bit about programming. Web development seems like the ultimate job when you're overly confident in your ability to turn on, and turn off the computer. However, one mention of the term 'programming', and it's all gibberish from there...However, this is only in your mind. You will find that after flirting with light programming (which HTML really is), you will be ready to hack into sophisticated computer networks such as the Blockbuster Video database, which is the only smart way of clearing past due video rentals from the record. Although HTML doesn't exactly teach you the principles necessary in moving billions of dollars from other more important people's off shore accounts into your piggy bank, it does however enable you to develop top of the line web sites. In fact, HTML (Hyper Text Markup Language) is the foundation to almost every web site on the Internet, and the best part is that it's easy to learn.

HTML was initially developed as a simple solution language for scientists and researchers who had not the slightest clue how to program a computer. The concept seemed simple enough to the Internet creators of the time. Basically they set out to create a language that could deliver simple application text with light formatting capabilities. In other words, they created the Geo Metro of the Internet.

As the Internet gained a new following of users other than those originally intended, designers on the web learned that they could essentially put Ferrari decals on the Geo Metro, and convince others it was truly a fast sports car. They had found a way to take a basic language and extend its vocabulary and range, so that it performed beyond what the creators ever imagined, even though the newer designed web sites were still developed in basic HTML.

If you are wondering what HTML looks like, the best way to accomplish this is to open your Internet Browser. In Netscape Communicator, visit any particular web site, then go to the top of the page, next choose the link called 'View', and finally, scroll down to 'Page Source'. A new window will open showing you all the HTML coding for whichever web page you happen to have been looking at in the Browser. In Microsoft Internet Explorer, visit any particular web site, then go to the top of the page, next choose the link called 'View', and finally, scroll down to 'Source'. You will once again be able to then view the HTML code for the page you were previously browsing.

2.2.3 Learning and Applying HTML

First off, don't be frightened by what you see. If you look close enough, you'll see that several of the elements in HTML are used over and over again. Next, you'll notice that there aren't a whole lot of numeric equations going on. This is because HTML is a text based language. This is a great thing for all those English wizards out there who never quite excelled at math. For instance, instead of saying something like E=MC2/*'a'*[((($null)||($NotNull))], just to get the letter 'a' to appear in italic bold text on the screen, you could simply say <I><b>a</b></I> in HTML. Although my E=MC2 example doesn't really come from an existing language, it does however give an idea as to how complex other source code languages can get. My goal is to draw your attention to the major difference in simplicity between most programming languages such as C++ and the basic HTML language. The <I> indicated italics, and the <b> indicated bold. The </I> indicated stop italics, and you guessed it! The </b> indicates stop bold. It's really that simple, and enclosed. All commands in HTML are surrounded by angle brackets, or to show you, the <

and the > symbols, while just plain text that you want to appear on the web site need no encapsulation by brackets or braces.

You should take note that all HTML pages are encapsulated. Not only by commands within angle bracketed shells, such as <b> for bold, but also as an entire page of code. For instance, if you start at the foundation of HTML scripting, you will notice that there are only about four major elements that make up a web page. The page would basically start with <html>, and if you scroll to the bottom of the page, it would close </html>. The rest of the site is then encapsulated within this first main statement.

Within <html> and </html> are <head><title>name goes here</title></head><body>and </body>. The <head> is where you generally add JavaScript and Jscript, which we'll cover further down the road, but you also would put the <title> here. Anything within <title> and </title> would appear as title text in the top left corner of the browser. Then everything else that consists of your web page content, including text, images, formatting, etc...would appear between the <body> and </body> tags. So that essentially you would have the following....

```
<html>
    <head>
            <title>
                    This Is My First Page
            </title>
    </head>
<body>
    blah, blah, blah...
</body>
</html>
```

You'll notice that I added tons of spaces, instead of using basic left justification. This is a valuable method of scripting and is considered standard formatting in the programming realm. It shows the mark of a true designer, and looks better, as it allows one to follow the basic syntax of a script. Readability should be one of the most sought after elements when developing HTML code. I recommend this because, when you develop a script, chances are extremely fair that it's not going to work as originally planned. It will usually require you having to check, modify, test, then recheck your coding until it is acceptable to you. Debugging good format-ted code is every programmer's dream come true.

You are probably now wondering how and where you go to start devel-oping your own HTML code. My answer to you is that it's closer to you than you might think. Although there are web site development kits that format the HTML for you, such as Microsoft FrontPage, Adobe Pagemill, Netscape Composer, and many others, I don't personally endorse these development tools. My reasoning is that until you get lots of 'hands on' experience with HTML, and dig right in the mud, you're never going to feel comfortable with HTML. Also, when you work in the Internet indus-try, although it's useful to know the different HTML development kits available to you, you'll find that you are often expected to create the code from scratch.

Just remember that Practice Makes Permanent! Once you've created a few web sites, the scripting portion of HTML will start coming natu-rally to you. With this little pep talk in mind, let's create our first HTML page together.

To create a web site, you need a pad to write the code on. No special software or program is necessary to accomplish this task. You are simply able to open any basic text editor such as Microsoft Word, or WordPad, BBEdit, or SimpleText. This is your new development environment for creating the ultimate in web entertainment. In the Industry, I use some-thing similar to WordPad, called VIM. VIM is a Visual (VI for short, orig-inally intended for UNIX environments) editor that allows you a higher level of debugging and scripting than a standard text editing program. However, a basic text editor is all we need to get started with.

Next, it's time to establish the shell that will encapsulate the bulk of our HTML code. Use the following example...

```
<html>
    <head>
            <title>
                    This Is My First Page
            </title>
    </head>
<body>
    <font face="arial, helvetica sans-serif" size="2">
    <b>This is my first website!</b>
    </font>
</body>
</html>
```

Notice the 'font face' tag? This specifically instructs the browser to display in the font type called arial. If the browser can not associate the text to that type, then it tries the next one, 'helvetica', and so on. The size indicates how large your text can be displayed. Also notice the order in which each tag is closed? The </font> closure didn't occur until the </b> closure, which is in sync with the order of operation.

It's important that you follow a few major rules when scripting. Although your script might still work without following these guidelines, it may not work universally on OTHER browsers. Only by following certains steps can you ensure that your bases are covered.

1) Always keep your scripts in lower case.

2) Always use good spacing technique. This keeps it easy to debug (debugging means that you are fixing errors).

3) Any tagged element that comes after an equal symbol should be surrounded by quotation marks. For instance, <font size="2">

4) Always close your tags in the proper order. For instance, if you have <font><I>, then make sure that they close from the inside out, so that </I></font>.

Now you should save your work. Like most other applications you might run on your computer, you should frequently save your work in case your computer gets bored, and decides to shut down on you just for the fun of watching you rant and rave over how you just lost hours of work because you forgot to save your progress. Look closely at your monitor when these little glitches occur. I didn't think it was possible for a computer to laugh, let alone laugh AT someone. I am now convinced that computers shut down for the sheer joy of watching people fuss.

When saving your progess, you will be asked what you would like to name the file, and where you would like to store it. You should definitely put the file somewhere that's easy to find later on. I've discovered several directories that would simply swallow my file whole, never to be found again, such as the toilet_bowl directory, and the black_hole directory…If you are ever unsure where to put a file, in fear that it will end up under your bed never to be found again, then I suggest that you place the file on your desktop (you can always move the file to another location later). When you give your new HTML script a file name, use a name that reflects the work such as internet_page (notice the underscore? You should never separate a web site filename with spaces. Instead, separate the words with an underscore.). Although you might not get a computer error for typing in a filename that's more than eight characters in length, you should keep it under this number for safety sake. End your filename with either the .html or .htm extension. This is how the browser interprets the file as an HTML document (For example, internet_page.html). There is no real difference between .htm and .html, except that some

ISP's require one over the other. Don't press the 'Okay' button just yet though, as there is one more task that must be completed in order for your browser to know that your file should be associated with the web. Look at the option for 'Save as Type'. You should ALWAYS set this to 'Text Only'. The reason for this is that any other setting could add additional non-valid characters to the script that although helpful for documents only being loaded by a word processor, could be damaging and come out full of errors when loaded with a web browser. Also, if you don't choose 'Text Only' or 'Plain Text' (depending on which word processor you are using), then it will not matter much that you've added .htm or .html to the end of the filename. Anything other than 'Text Only' or 'Plain Text' will have a default extension added behind your .htm or .html extension, which would also cause errors (for instance, internet_page.html.doc would occur if I left the "Save as Type' value set on 'Word Document' instead of 'Text Only' or 'Plain Text').

The next task is to open your browser and view the locally saved change. I say locally saved, because you didn't save this file on another computer other than your own. Even though you will be viewing your page on an Internet Web Browser, don't be fooled. This doesn't mean that your page is now viewable by the entire world of users. It simply means that you are going to load a local page into your browser for private viewing. Your page couldn't be viewed by another until you moved the file to your actual web site storage space, on the server hosted by whichever ISP or Network Provider you have chosen to do business with.

Open your browser. If a new window prompts you to connect to the Internet, simply click on the button marked 'cancel'. This will not close your browser window. Then move your cursor over the 'File' option at the top of the screen, and scroll down to 'Open'. Then choose 'Browse', and hunt down the HTML file, where ever it may be hiding (the desktop is always a worthwhile place to check). A path will then appear that points to this file, where ever it might be residing on your hard drive. Click on the 'Okay' button, and whalla, your web site will then load amidst fireworks and the Mormon Tabernacle Choir singing "Hallelujah!"…At about this point, you will probably wonder why your web site looks nothing like Disney's or one of the other super neat web sites that are floating out there in that great expanse of open digital space. All I can say is patience my little grasshopper. Rome wasn't built in a day, nor will you be convincing others that your Geo Metro is a turbo charged sports car until you can prove it with neat little Ferrari decals stuck everywhere.

I would love to devote my time and energy into instructing you further on HTML, but I'm afraid that my main focus in this book is to get you prepped for a great job! HTML is only one of several tools that web designers must know in order to create suave and hip web sites on the net. It's important that you devote time to studying and applying HTML though, as most of your web work with encompass the use of this language. Therefore, I will give you several references that will assist you in the arena of scripting HTML. Just remember that regardless of how much HTML coding a web site might contain, it can easily be broken down into encapsulated pieces that are not as menacing to look at. Remember that you can learn a great deal, simply by viewing a web pages source code. If you like a particular web page, it's usually a great tool to see how they accomplished it, then going back to your text editor and trying to copy what they did. And remember the importance of HTML. Without a strong understanding of this language, you're not going to get far as a web designer. In many ways, it can be compared to trying to get a job as a translator for a foreign language that you have never learned. You could always fudge your way into it, and make it up as you go, but at some point, you've simply got to know the language to make it work. But don't fret over it. HTML is one of the most simple languages to learn. It's text based, and extremely versatile. It's compact, and even fits comfortably in the glove compartment!

Here is a list of web resources that will assist you in learning HTML. These resources are freely available to users on the Internet (however, if you prefer, you can send me a lot of money for these resources and I'll be sure to forward it to the proper place, with a no money back guarantee!)...

http://hotwired.lycos.com/webmonkey/teachingtool/

http://www.builder.com

http://www.w3.org/

You can also visit your local bookstore and purchase 'HTML: The Definitive Guide, 3rd

Edition' by Chuck Musciano (O'Reilly & Associates), which covers all the essentials to developing in the HTML format.

2.2.4 HTTP & HTTPS

HTTP stands for Hyper Text Transfer Protocol. This is the method in which web site data finds it's way to your browser from the web (or WWW) server (for instance, *http://www.blahblahblah.com*). It's considered the standard transport method when downloading web site content. A long time ago in a galaxy far, far away...The HTTP protocol was primarily meant to load the contents of a web page by making a TCP/IP (Transport Control Protocol/ Internet Protocol) connection to the server for EVERY image and bit of content it had to load. a TCP/IP connection is where your browser makes a request for information from the server, which takes awhile when you consider that the server must take a few nanoseconds to find the information and send it back via the IP address (we covered this earlier. Remember 207.217.102.122 instead of *http://www.blahblahblah.com*? This is the IP part of TCP/IP). This was fine however, all the way until the ice age when someone discovered a new HTTP 'keep-alive' function that enabled a terminal (your computer) to keep it's connection with the server (the storage shed) until all the little buttons, graphics, and animations were fully downloaded. This cut latency dramatically (it sped up the process!). Most servers and browsers now support HTTP 1.0 or higher, which is what utilizes the keep-alive feature.

HTTPS indicates that you are about to visit a web site page that is strictly Secured (Hyper Text Transfer Protocol Secure). Usually a web page is secured because the page is going to ask you for sensitive information, such as credit card information. Any information is consider unsafe and easily viewable by the world on the Internet, including by all those poorly starved Ohio State University students that would love to get a hold of your credit card information so they can make a chips & dip run to the supermarket. Although I've never actually heard of this happening, I can attest to eagerly wanting people's credit card numbers for this purpose when I was in school. Anyway, the web page is secured because the page utilizes a type of SSL (Secure Socket Layer) that takes the credit card numbers you type in and spits out gibberish encrypted meaningless phrases such as 'toad lawyer expense paid vacation llamas groovy party'. These Pig Latin phrases make it's way back to the server, where they are then safely decrypted by PGP software (Pretty Good Protection) back into their original form, which in this particular case would translate into 'groovy llamas paid toad lawyer vacation party expenses'. This is a great way to keep sensitive information such as waist sizes and denture filling dates hidden from the spying eyes of the 'Global Village' of Internet users. One way to tell that the page is secure, is to check the URL. Make sure that it says *https://www.feefifofum.com*. Another way, is to look in the lower left corner of your browser. Any page that is secured will display a lock that is in the locked mode, or a key that is not broken, and is shining in gold. If you see any dancing llamas go across your screen though, then this is a strong indication that you should refrain from using the browser any longer. Computers infested by digital llamas can prove to be extremely difficult in removing. Your best bet in casting these demons out of your computer is to send a gratuitous donation to my home address, in which case, they will move on to your neighbors computer, where this vicious cycle will repeat itself again and again.

2.2.5 Macromedia Shockwave & Flash Technology

Many web sites offer a little more pizzazz to their content. Instead of the static bland page that has text and graphics, there are now sites that utilize Macromedia technology to spice things up a little. With Macromedia, a web page can come to life with smooth animation that is interactive and usually mixed with groovy music and sound effects. Dynamic multimedia content provided by Shockwave or Flash can add much needed intensity to a web site that might otherwise be dull and boring. For instance, Hollywood uses this format to add flavor to web sites promoting anticipated movies. They'll usually include games, and an environmental element that throws the user into the movie. Scary movie web sites might add distant sound effects such as wind and thunder that grow louder as your cursor moves closer to an image or link, while other movies might add text that blurs and fades to the sound of a jazzy tune.

Macromedia applications cannot run on a browser without the necessary plug-in installed before hand. The plug-in enables the browser to incorporate multimedia files into a web page, and is freely available at *http://www.macromedia.com.* If you decide to build a web page with these extended features, it's usually in your best interest to offer a splash page before you get to the actual home page (which is to say, the main page). The splash page should ask the user whether they would like to view the enhanced site (including Macromedia glitter and gold), or the lite version of the site (very basic, containing rusty cranks and shafts from the precambrian era). Also, the splash page should offer a link to Macromedia where the user can download the latest and greatest version of Shockwave or Flash. Just keep in mind though, that many people get upset with splash pages. This is most especially true when they have spent hours waiting for the page content to load, only to be told that they now get to choose which version of the home page they'd like to have loaded next. This usually tends to bring out the tension in people, and is the most probable reason that monitors fly out of office windows by accident or in extreme circumstances, brand new computers are sold at garage sales for $1.50. Another terrific solution to adding Flash content, is to offer it as a compliment to your web page. In other words, skip the splash page, offer a link from your home page asking if you want to see the snazzy Flash enhanced information.

To Develop a Macromedia Shockwave or Flash application, you would need to purchase Macromedia Director for Shockwave rich-media applications, or Macromedia Flash/Freehand Studio, for (you guessed it!) Flash applications. This is the program that contains the tools necessary in creating plush content. You would also need to learn another language called Lingo, for which many 'How To' guides are available. Lingo offers flexible features in developing smooth multimedia transitions, or at least this is what the Macromedia sales agent told me. I seem to recall that my used car sales agent told me the exact same thing right before I drove away in my sparkling, (almost) new Cheverolet Vega. I would suggest that you take a multimedia class or read up on these interactive utilities though, before tackling the complexities of animation and dynamic content. I would also strongly suggest that you bring a lawyer, mechanic and multimedia college professor before you visit a used car lot.

Although there are many differences between Shockwave and Flash, you can ultimately create either type of application with Macromedia Director. Let's take a quick moment to go over the differences between Shockwave and Flash.

Macromedia Shockwave: Provides seamless rich-media content to the browser. Applications of this type are created with Macromedia Director, which requires functional use of the Lingo programming language. You won't need to know quantum physics or underwater basket weaving to figure this language out, but like most things in life, it's easy to learn yet hard to master. You can create executable programs that are self contained (meaning that they will run as a stand-alone applications) away from the browser. For instance, several video games are made using Macromedia Shockwave, and can be played from a CD, having nothing to do with the Internet. More than likely, you will need to download and install the Shockwave Player and plug-in to enable the product to work. Over 30 million people have successfully downloaded the necessary Shockwave player to view this medium.

Macromedia Flash: A vector based application that creates smooth animations with soft blended edges (this feature is called anti-aliased). Unlike Shockwave which must load the entire file before playing it, Flash on the other hand delivers speed since it can play a file while it's in the download process. Over 222 million people currently have the ability to use the Flash technology as it comes 'built-in' with most major software packages distributed by Earthlink Network, AOL, Netscape, Microsoft, Apple, Gateway and Disney among others.

2.2.6 JavaScript, JScript & JAVA. There's a difference?!

As you learn more about HTML, you'll find that for being a generalized markup language, it's not exactly turbo charged. There's no real umph in HTML, as a stand—alone scripting language. Think of it as a fireplace. HTML provides the perfect hearth for crackling a warm fire on a cold winter's day, but without the logs, you're not going to get exactly what you were hoping for. The logs are a lot like Java. Java is an additional language that can be used with HTML, to heat things up a bit. You can use Java applications to add more flexibility to your content such as color management, animation, sound effects that occur only when you roll the mouse cursor over certain links or text, images that highlight when the mouse cursor rolls over them, programs that change dirty diapers, etc...

The problem with Java though is that it comes in many different flavors, so it's important that you know the differences. As a web designer, chances are extremely good that you will run into either a Java based application, JAVA applet, or JavaScript coding embedded in the HTML source code. Your choices are between JavaScript, JScript and JAVA. WARNING: JAVA is not JavaScript, or JScript.

JavaScript was created to add more powerful functionality to HTML without having to require an actual programmer to accomplish the same goals with C++, which is a highly powerful programming language that is spoken mostly in equations. If you thought French was a difficult foreign language to learn, you should listen to a conversation about functions and logic in C++. For example...

John: Did you set the numeric integers null before you compiled the steam generated dual enhanced micro carbon flouride?

Bill: No, I found that if I simply deleted the non-linear escape character on the Parem statement, it executed the binary with a bit of garlic.

JavaScript is a product of Netscape, so it's natural to assume that Microsoft would HAVE to reinvent the wheel, and create a reverse engineered version of JavaScript, called JScript. They are both similar enough that differences shouldn't pose problems, but there are the occasional commands that one may understand over the other. To this end, several books now exist that outline their major differences for programming benefit. Both JavaScript and JScript are downloaded with the web page and then interpreted by the browser, therefor they are slaves to the HTML coding (although HTML is far inferior), or known as 'browser-dependent'. There are still some browsers that don't interpret JavaScript or JScript, however the major browsers such as Netscape Communicator and Microsoft Internet Explorer do, so a majority of the Internet users have the ability to use these extended features on their browsers. If you wanted to find Javascript or JScript in the Source Code, you would simply need to find <script> and </script> in the HTML source code. Whatever resides within these encapsulated tags would contain the essentials of the JavaScript or JScript coding.

JAVA is quite a bit different (just the fact that it's all in upper-case should be enough to convince you!). JAVA has to be compiled into .class files with a JAVA compiler (a compiler is a data cruncher. It takes a file and reformats it into a compressed version of the original so that it executes only as the file it's intended to be. For instance, before you compile a JAVA applet script, you could open the file with a word processor to view the coding. However, once it's compiled, it's not meant to run on a word processor any longer, so it might look like gibberish...). You would need to embed a reference to the .class script by adding an <applet> tag to the HTML script. Then when the web page loads on the client's browser, the .class file would need to load as a separate script, which would then close with </applet>. Also, when you get into the more professional realm of web design, you might find yourself tinkering with HTML templates that are parsed by a JAVA engine using JSP (Java Server Pages) consisting of servlets, which are little elves that tinker files together on the server.

You should know that there are different versions of JavaScript and JScript. This is about as important as knowing how many cylinders your auto engine has, and what the torque ratio is, and how much horsepower it can muster as well. Why, you ask? Because there's always that ONE person, that's going to have nothing better to do then to say, 'Ah, JavaScript! What version are you using?! And how much torque does the horsepower ratio have in it's cylinders?!'...Anyway, it's important, so I'm going to tell you. Although I don't think this needs to be memorized, I do think you should have a general idea how the product version convention works, so when someone DOES (heaven forbid) ask you what version you're using, you don't sputter confidently about how you're using the quad chasi, ecto-plasmic, three liter, dual piston, singularly mounted, inferno torqued ver-sion of JavaScript 3000x. So then, here goes the versions convention....

JavaScript 1.0 was first supported in Netscape Navigator 2.0 (which came WAY before Netscape Communicator!). Netscape Navigator 3.0 supports JavaScript 1.1, and Netscape Communicator supports JavaScript 1.1 and 1.2...Then there's JScript, which is extremely similar. It's a good thing that Microsoft used the term 'reverse engineering' on JScript. It just sounds so much better than copy infringement. In actuality, the legend says that once upon a time, Netscape was slow in getting the JavaScript specifications to Microsoft, so they simply created their own version.

It's a great idea to know how all three languages work and function, especially come resume time, but out of the three, the most emphasis should be placed on learning JavaScript. It's more widely used than JAVA applets or JScript. Plus, chances are fair that you won't need to alter your JavaScript coding much to fit the requirements on Microsoft Internet Explorer to get it in sync with JScript. If you would like to learn more about these three languages, you can go to *http://www.yahoo.com* and search for 'JavaScript tutorials'. I'll give you a head start though, and send you to *http://www.webdeveloper.com* or *http://www.builder.com* where you will find examples of JavaScript, JAVA applets, and JScript as well as guides on how to create Java coding, including examples. If you'd like some relax-ing reading on Javascript, I would suggest 'Javascript: The Definitive Guide, 3rd Edition' by David Flanagan (O'Reilly & Associates).

2.2.7 CGI and PERL

CGI does NOT stand for Cows Gone Indigo, but it DOES stand for Common Gateway Interface. The Gateway Interface is a way of bringing server-side scripts created with programming languages such as PERL (Practical Extraction and Report Language) or SHELL, together with HTML client-side scripts (remember that client side is the computer at home that makes the initial dial up connection to the server via the Internet). The CGI scripts are external, and create a 'Gateway' interface between external source of data and the server. CGI enables input and output of data from the front-end to the back-end (another way of saying from the client-side to the server-side, which is another way of saying from your home computer to the server), and vice-versa. For instance, if you wanted to authenticate credit card information over a web page, you would need to ask the user for their credit card information (which would then be transported via CGI, or the Gateway, to the backend, where a PERL script would execute and run an authentication against the credit card. The PERL script would then output HTML to the client-side browser once the routine was completed. PERL is used for form submissions (forms are a good way of collecting information on users such as where they are from, how they heard about the site, what their email address is or anything else you might find useful), counter displays (how many people hit your web site today?), credit card authentication (E-commerce), and many other functions as well. Sometimes entire web sites are built out of PERL, and other times the functions that you might expect to be built in PERL are actually built using JavaScript, JScript, or JAVA!

Not all ISP's or Network Providers that provide web services, offer manual PERL or SHELL executable compiling ability on the back-end, or server-side (which is bad, because if it ain't compiled, it ain't gonna run...). This is for security reasons, as there are some bad seeds out there called 'hackers' that make it their sole purpose to make life difficult for Server Administrators. Great caution must always go into maintaining servers as they cost so darned much to setup in the first place. It's always a good idea to check before you setup an account, as to whether you'll have CGI or JAVA support from their servers. Usually, you'll find greater restrictions on free web sites, and much more versatile support on the paid web sites.

PERL can be written in a standard word processor, but it looks more like C++, then HTML and it can't be tested until it's been compiled. JAVA for that matter also looks similar to PERL. If you would like your very own copy of PERL for testing purposes, then visit the following location, download and then install the application. *http://www.activestate.com*. You can find the most comprehensive instructions on it's versatility and usefulness from this location.

When scripting in PERL, it's important to note a couple of things. First, a PERL script almost always begins with the first line reading #!/usr/bin/perl, which is where PERL is usally installed on a server. If your ISP or Network Provider has installed PERL in a different directory, then this first line would need to be changed to the proper location. The script will not work, if it can't find the installed components. Also, PERL script files end in the .pl extension. This is a great way to know what kind of file you'll be looking at as a web designer.

Here are a list of basic extensions to know…

.htm or .html—HTML files

.class—JAVA applet files

.js—JavaScript files (although JavaScript does not have to be saved in a separate file. This is mostly used when segmenting certain code that can be called for over and over again in HTML, without having to rewrite it redundantly over and over again.)

.pl—PERL scripts for CGI

.sh—SHELL scripts which can be written for CGI instead of PERL.

Also, what's good to note is that if you are debugging a PERL script, and want to see whether the script outputs HTML coding (which can be run straight from a PERL script), you would simply need to find the following line…

```
print "Content-type: text/html\n\n";
```

Everything after this line should look strangely familiar as it will be HTML tags embedded within the gateway script. Notice also that the line above has a semi-colon (;) at the end of it? This is how every line in a PERL script should end. Usually, HTML is embedded in PERL to accomplish a thank you page after a form has been submitted. For instance, you are on a page that asks you questions. You press the submit button, and a new page appears saying "thanks, we got your form". This second page would have been generated by the external CGI program after collecting the data from the form. Then the gateway would be closed and would revert to HTML files again.

2.2.8 Apple Quicktime Vs. Microsoft Media Player

If you haven't guessed it yet, Apple Computers and Microsoft Corporation are not the best of friends. Apple Computers was started by Steve Jobs and Steve Wozniak, with some friends, out of a suburban garage in California. After having stumbled across some toys produced by the Xerox Corporation, such as the Mouse (not the furry little creature, mind you...We're talking more specifically about the computer device!), and a GUI Operating System (GUI stands for Graphic User Interface. This meant that the screen was filled with friendly graphical windows and icons to make computing easier...), Apple created the ultimate user friendly computer system called the Macintosh, that left a trail of dust all over IBM. Considering that IBM was the only other computer manufacturer that could potentially hurt Apple's sales, it's no wonder that Apple saw IBM as the ULTIMATE enemy. After all, Apple Computers represented a new way of thinking out of the corporate box. Steve Jobs walked around the Silicon Valley based Apple Head Quarters barefoot and in shorts. At IBM, People dressed in business suites, worked in cubicles and sang company songs (they actually knew the words by heart!).

All the while, and unbeknownst to Apple Computers, there was a little company based in Seattle called Microsoft that was preparing for war. Started by Bill Gates and Paul Allen, Microsoft went to the goliath IBM Corporation and offered them a Disk Operating System (Called DOS for short) for their new computer that would compete against Apple. The only catch in the deal presented by Microsoft, was that Bill Gates wanted to keep the license to DOS for distribution purposes, instead of selling it over to IBM. After very brief considerable thought, IBM decided that the money was in the hardware and not the software, so they agreed to Microsoft's request, and purchased the first Disk Operating System from the small company called Microsoft, while allowing Microsoft to retain ownership rights to the software (Whoops!). What soon followed can only be described as a very, VERY expensive mistake on the part of IBM. It turned out that software was worth more than the Computer hardware that ran it. This is where Microsoft became a thorn in the side of Apple Computers and became the largest company in the world with an annual cash flow equivalent to the GDP of such little countries as, oh…THE UNITED STATES!

Steve Jobs was so busy trying to develop the ultimate windows based computer, that he didn't see the impending threat by Microsoft. Bill Gates had created DOS for the IBM computer line, but it wasn't based on a GUI design. It was text based, difficult to use, and required the user to know what a C:> prompt meant (by the way, the C:> is the command line prompt that tells you it's okay to start typing…). So, Bill Gates took from Apple Computers, what Apple had taken from Xerox, and he created the first IBM compatible GUI based, Windows environment. Needless to say, Steve Jobs was not terribly happy about that, since it pretty much brought IBM up-to-date and side by side with Apple on the computer front.

Apple Computers took a serious turn for the worse after that. Steve Jobs was fired, and their stock price dropped heavily. All this happened while Microsoft flourished. Bill Gates strategically led Microsoft into the most powerful company in the World by developing Windows upgrades, from Windows version 3.1 and Windows 98 to Windows 2000. Steve Jobs has since gone back to Apple Computers, and has been praised for bringing them back into the light. He's been key in the development of the IMac Computer (think jellyfish...) and the Apple Cube (their newest computer invention, and might I add the Porsche of all computers), which once again has Apple revolutionizing the digital marketplace.

Now that you've had a quick rundown on the bitter history between these two rivals, it should become a little more clear as to why there is fierce product competition between them. In this particular case, Apple Computers created Quicktime for the Internet browser, which enables a computer to receive video and audio files from the World Wide Web. Quicktime enables a user to watch movie or television broadcast clips over the Internet. Microsoft Media Player does the same thing. Apple Quicktime and Microsoft Media Player work on both Apple computers and PC compatible computers, while also able to work on various browsers. In either case, the user must first install the media player on their system, before their browser can interpret the video and audio files correctly. As a web designer, you should know about file streaming. When a file streams, it can play at any time while the file is still downloading. Of course, as a web designer, it also helps to know why IBM PC users hate the APPLE Mac users, and vice versa...

2.2.9 Graphics: .gif vs. .jpg

When you view images on the Internet, it's important to note that there are different types of images that are used for different types of situations. The two main types of graphic file formats are GIF and JPEG.

GIF—has the .gif file extension (for example, imagename.gif). The Graphics Interchange format was developed in the 1980's by Compuserve (another network provider), and is most commonly used for transparencies (where you can see through parts of the image, to the layer beneath it), animations and line art. Generally, you would want to use the GIF format when you don't mind your image palette being able to only handle 256 colors at a single time since it can only handle an 8 bit-depth display. Also, you can create some pretty snazzy animated sequences that stream since GIF provides a multiblock solution where separate blocks can store separate images within a single file, giving the illusion of movement (like flipping pages of a book that have a slight change on each page).

JPEG—has the .jpg file extension (for example, imagename.jpg). The Joint Photographic Experts Group format is most commonly used to display photographic images that contain millions of colors (24 bit-depth capable) more than the restrictive GIF format that can only utilize up to 256 colors simultaneously. JPEG retains all the color information by providing a choice in compression methods, compresses the image then has to decompress the image before it can be viewed. A higher compression level provides lower image quality and a smaller file size, while a lower compression level provides much better image quality but a higher file size (and not to mention a longer download period as well).

Also, when you script a page that will be calling for the use of images, you should make sure to always use the 'height' and 'width' attributes of the <img src> tag to restate the image's actual dimensions. This enables the browser to render the rest of the page while the image is still downloading. If you leave out the 'height' and 'width' attributes, then the page will remain blank until every last image is loading, thus causing the user to shake the monitor violently until exhaustion forces them to simply give up and wait aimlessly for the entire page to load.

2.2.10 Adobe Photoshop & Illustrator and other graphic utilities

Developing graphics for the Internet is a pretty major part of being a web designer, especially when one of your main concerns is the web site interface, and layout of the page. Graphic design can involve the manipulation of current images, creating images from scratch, creating logos, banners, backgrounds, icons, anti-aliased (or smoothed) title text with no jagged edges, resizing photographs, reformatting color schemes on existing images, optimizing image resolutions for best quality while maintaining the smallest possible file size, providing layout sketches and mockups (otherwise known as screen shots) plus a number of other things. But the one point I can't make clear enough, is that you will need to have solid knowledge of a graphics program that can help you accomplish these tasks in order to succeed as a web designer.

There are many graphic programs available, and each has unique abilities, but you should start saving your pennies now, so you can purchase Adobe Photoshop and Adobe Illustrator. Unlike other graphic programs available in the market, these two programs are considered the industry standard by professionals in digital media.

These programs are expensive though, costing upward of three hundred dollars per program. But your money couldn't be better spent on any other alternative. Adobe Photoshop gives you the power of retouching photograph proofs, original or composite artwork, collages, photo montages, and is exceptional as a mockup tool for creating exact web site examples before you begin the process of creating the actual HTML for the page. Adobe Photoshop creates raster (otherwise known as bitmap) images, made from a grid of tiny squares called pixels to represent the image. Every single pixel is given a color value and exact location. Because the image is bitmapped or pixel based, it's considered to be resolution-dependent. This means that the image can loose detail and appear jagged if viewed at a high magnification level. However, pixel based graphics are best at displaying subtle gradations of shades and color. As a web designer who has the responsibility of creating a web site from start to finish, you will more than likely utilize most of the tools found in Adobe Photoshop throughout the entire web site building process, from conception, to the finished product.

Adobe Illustrator is a great tool for developing vector graphics, which are made of lines and curves defined by mathematical objects called vectors. Graphics created in Ilustrator are not bitmapped or defined by small pixel squares, therefore it's considered to be resolution-independent, because you can scale the magnification of the image without loosing detail or clarity. This is a great application for creating logos, or crisp icon graphics that must retain sharp lines when scaled to various sizes.

Although Adobe makes both programs, and they utilize many of the same characteristics, they are however very different programs with very different purposes. For example, Adobe Illustrator wouldn't be the best choice for editing a photograph, as it's not able to define the photograph into independent shapes and objects, such as circles and squares. Photograph retouching would be best if done in Adobe Photoshop, where the image is converted into an RGB raster (bitmapped) image that's made up of extremely small pixel squares that are defined an exact color and coordinate.

So you see, there are several tools to choose from when it comes time to building the web site. I've only briefly touched on the surface of what's available for building web sites. If you take some time to browse *http://www.tucows.com* or *http://www.builder.com*, you will find additional resources for developing on the web. The advantage for you in working with different mediums (tools), is that you will have much more to talk about in your Dot Com job interview. Plus, it really helps spice up your resume!

2.3 Making the Schematics

So far, so good. We've found a great home for our new web site, and we've discovered that there are many tools we can use to build the structure with. Next comes the fun part, which of course is hiring a contractor to finish the job for you...No! That's not right, but it sure would make life easier wouldn't it? Actually, it's time to decide what we want our new structure to look like.

2.3.1 Making a web plan

As a web designer, it's hard to resist the urge to just jump into a project and start building the site from scratch, using imagination and experience to make the ultimate web site. Although this is a good gung-ho approach, it's unfortunately not the best way to create a professional web site, especially for a pre-IPO Dot Com company.

It's extremely important that you sit down and chart out a path for your web site content, so that you might create a plan that serves as a road map to how your site functions, what it accomplishes and how it behaves.

Your plan should start with a mission statement or goal, so that you have an accomplishable finish line. I am a firm believer that a web site is always a work in progress, because it's always being reevaluated and redesigned and appended to as technology changes. But, I also believe that it's important to set goals that can be reached so that you can gauge your progress.

Let's role-play for a moment, so I can give you real world examples when developing a web schematic. You've just been hired by Billy Joe's Tuna Tacos Stand, to create the ultimate web site presence on the Internet. You've spoken with your new client and have found that Billy Joe wants a family oriented happy themed web site with pictures of their fine Tuna Taco products, and the ability to show television commercials as well. The only problem is that he doesn't have digital pictures, images, or graphic logos for you to use, so you're on your own.

Now that you're on your own, it's time to evaluate what you can do to help create the most spectacular web site for your new client.

2.3.2 Using Visio and other flow chart applications

Although you can sketch out a flow chart with pen and paper, you should be comfortable using products such as Visio (a flow chart program). Flow chart programs can help sort out the complications of navigation management for a web site that's in progress. For instance, Billy Joe's Tuna Tacos Stand web site should have more than just a Home Page to accomplish all the tasks that have been requested by the client. Let's go over some reasons as to why you should sketch out a flow chart.

1. It provides you with an overview as to how deep your site takes a user. Users don't like to have to dig their way to information on a web site. The majority of Internet users want their information quickly and easily. That usually means having to keep a web site from having too many levels.

   Level 1

   Home Page—with links to a 'Company Info' page, and 'Products' page

   Level 2

   Company Info Page—with links to 'About Us' and 'Job Opportunities', and back to Level 1

   Products Page—with links to 'What we sell' and 'How we sell it', and back to Level 1

   Level 3

   About Us Page—links back to Level 1 and Level 2

Job Opportunities Page—links back to Level 1 and Level 2

What We Sell Page—links back to Level 1 and Level 2

How We Sell It Page—links back to Level 1 and Level 2

2. A flow chart can give you an indication as to how long the project might take to complete. For instance, if it takes you three days of development time to create a single page, then you have a rough idea as to the overall project time. (as a professional web designer, you should be able to complete a web page in under 3 to 5 hours. This figure is only based on scripting and debugging, and not on creating new images. The images should be given about 3 to 5 hours to create and prepare for their transfer to the webpage). This information can be crucial for a client who is paying by the hour, or by the page. Of course, you can always use the mechanics approach, which is to multiply the estimated completion time by a factor of twelve, then take a vacation with all the free time.

3. It can assist you in brainstorming for content ideas. Once you have an overview of all the components that will make up the web site, it's much easier to see in detail whether additional pieces might be needed to help create a more presentable web site.

4. It serves as an aid for mapping what tools you will need for which segmented web pages displayed. For instance, if you know that the client will want animation, you can plot out where the animation will be most effective, which program you will create the animation with, and how much of the site will be devoted to this type of functionality.

In the case of Billy Joe's Tuna Tacos Stand web site, you've found that your flow chart works as follows:

Level 1

Home Page—links to 'Company Info', 'Products', 'Commercials', and 'Kids Only'

Level 2

Company Info—links to Level 1, 'About Us' and 'Jobs'

Commercials—links to Level 1

Kids Only—links to Level 1, 'Games' and 'Did You Know?'

Level 3

About Us—Links to Level 1 and Level 2

Jobs—Links to Level 1 and Level 2

Games—Links to Level 1 and Level 2

Did You Know?—Links to Level 1 and Level 2

This hierarchy now enables you to negotiate a contract price based on the amount of time it will take to complete (In this case, let's figure about 3 days per page, and you're creating 8 pages which equates to A LOT OF MONEY!!!). Billy Joe has signed off on your flow, which prepares you to move into the next phase which is...

2.3.3 Quick Sketches and Paper Napkins

This is absolutely the best part of the process! You get to take your shoes off, put your feet in the pool, and sun bathe with your shades on while you draw quick sketches that represent how you will format the web pages. This is where your creative talents can shine the most. There will be times during this process where a page layout idea will hit you with clarity, and of course you will be at Denny's munching on a breakfast buffet when it hits you. Don't fret, just grab the nearest tree made or recycled paper product (most likely a paper napkin), and sketch away! Don't worry about mistakes, because these are layout drafts, and will probably be appended over and over again until you get the layout just right.

For instance, do you put the hyperlinks in a vertical table to the left, while providing pictures and content in a vertical table to the right, with a logo at the top, and a footer with hyperlinks at the bottom? Or do you put the hyperlinks horizontally across the top of the page directly to the right of the logo, using all of the available lower space for content and images? Are the pages shaped like Volvos with sharp edges, or does it look more fluid with rounded corners?...There are many different ways to present a web page. The only true way to see which methods work, is to browse the Internet for awhile. Take some time to pay special attention to how each company web site is laid out. There are many different designs, and they all work to some extent fairly well. I'll give you good professional advice though and tell you that you should think out of the box. Try several different approaches. Sometimes, there's more than one answer for the problem, in which case you can present several different mockups of the same page to your client, who can then make the ultimate decision.

2.3.4 Making graphical mockups

I especially enjoy this process as much as the last. Although You won't be sunbathing during this portion of development (unless you're on a laptop, in which I hate you because I do not have a laptop), you will be utilizing your newly acquired graphic development skills with Adobe Photoshop.

Making mockups can be challenging, but in a fun way. You literally get to develop your napkin art into truly sophisticated screenshots of what exactly the finished project will look like, complete with all the trimmings.

It's best to have a good quality laser jet color printer available, as you'll need to print out copies of each mockup both for the client and for your portfolio. These printed copies will go to your client for approval, where your client will then take a ball point pen and mark all over your new work of art with requested additions and changes. Get used to this, as you will go through this process several times. The process is called Revision. You will go back and forth with the graphically adjusted changes until it looks just right, in which case your client will sign off on the page, and you will move to a mockup of the next page. This should happen for every page that must be created to complete an entire web site. Not only does it keep your client in the loop, but it helps ensure that you are developing exactly what's been requested of you. Also, it's pretty darned important to note that when you mockup a page, you should make sure you are developing at 72 dpi (dots per inch) which is what an average monitor displays, as this is how it would appear (in an accurate scale of 1:1) on the browser. Finally, you should work only with a web safe color palette of 256 colors. You can definitely choose to use colors from the grand selection of 16 million colors or more, but in actuality, the web browser will just convert the colors to one of 216 browser-safe colors anyway if the user has a standard 8 bit (256 color) monitor display, which could be devastating if your intention was a creamy broccoli green, and you got neon brown instead. Most users only have 8 bit monitors (since that's the most generic and fair priced display), while you as the web designer will probably want a 24 bit or higher display since 24 bit is necessary when wanting to display 16 million colors or more.

If you'd like to learn more about web safe color palettes or creating graphics that are perfect for the web, I would really suggest that you visit your local book store and purchase 'Coloring Web Graphics—The Definitive Resource for Color on the Web' by Lynda Weinman and Bruce Heavin, and published by New Riders (1996).

2.3.5 Cover your bases

The whole point for setting up a flow chart, layout sketches, and graphical mockups are to ensure that you've covered your bases in the initial phase of development. It's easy to jump into a project by skipping these steps, but it ultimately leads to disappointment, frustration, and friction between you (as the designer) and your client. The client wants immediate results, and taking these additional precautions before building the web site structure keeps them happily in the loop. It also ensures that you are developing a web site to meet all the specifications. It should be obvious that you're going to probably miss some of the details until after you start testing the finalized HTML version of the web site, but that will be minimal when compared to the damages that might be done if you developed around these steps.

2.4 How Firm a Foundation

Since you now have a schematic of the building, a place to build, and some general tools to build with, you can now take a breather before the construction begins, and take a walk around the lot to view the scene. This is a good time to start taking into consideration some pointers to building a web site.

2.4.1 Building within size constraints

The Internet reminds me of sitting in a really fast sports car, stuck behind a tractor going one mile an hour with no way to drive around it. This is because when you load some web sites onto your browser, it can take anywhere between one minute and one year to load a single page. There are a couple of reasons why this is, and it's vital that you take these pointers into consideration when constructing your web site. After all, people will only wait so long for a web page to load until mass hysteria sets in and forces entire countries to revert to a retro version of the 70's including disco halls, bell bottoms pants, and acres of computer junkyards.

The first major issue is modem speed. Most people connect to the Internet from a standard analog phone line. A browser sends a request through the modem, to the server for data. The server then sends the data back to the browser via the phone line. The problem with this is that phone lines can only move compressed data packets so fast before corruption occurs. If the data packets become corrupted, then the browser will keep nagging the server until it gets the whole enchilada, which is to say, data packets that aren't broken. Phone lines are very touchy as well. A single gust of wind is enough to create static and line noise that can corrupt data packets which are in transit. Also, data can generally only move up to 56 kilobytes of data per second (also called 56k or 56kb). Most people have a 56k modem, which means they have the means necessary in receiving data at the higher speeds, but other factors usually slow the transfer back down to an average 33.6 kilobytes per second. Some people even use modems that are only equipped to reach blistering speeds of up to 24.4k or 33.6k.

Some people connect from their homes to speeds of either ISDN, Cable modems, DSL, and Fractional or Frame Relay (T1 through T3). The problem with these faster connections for a web designer, is that there aren't enough people connected to them. If people can't receive data at a fairly quick rate, it kind of makes Web Developing obsolete. Prices are becoming more reasonable for DSL (Digital Subscriber Line), Cable Modem connections, and ISDN, but the majority of Internet users are not familiar enough with the different types of connections to make a financially sound decision one way or another. In the meantime, web designers will simply have to take extra precautions in developing groovy sites that load quick enough even for those with extremely slow modem speeds.

Another major issue is net congestion. If you haven't guessed it yet, the Internet swarms with millions of people every second of every day, and the number of connections to the net are going up. As more and more people connect to the same web pages at the same time, servers will have a harder time transferring data to everyone all at once. In fact, I have a very strong feeling that the Internet will naturally morph into a virtual waiting room where some virtual artificial intelligence named Helga will bark at you to "Take a number, sit down, shut up and wait your turn!". This could very well be the definitive solution that wins me the Nobel Prize.

Take for example an episode where hackers pushed congestion to the extreme, and generally made life difficult for everyone, for an entire day! Several hackers (people that break into systems that aren't meant to be broken into, cause mischief, tamper with intellectual property, plant computer viruses and frequently spend their free time eating twinkies.) sent a 'ping' command to servers for CNN, Amazon, Ebay and other major sites over and over again. A 'ping' command, is when you send a request to a server to make sure it's alive and well. The server responds to these pings by bouncing the signal, much in the way that sonar bounces off the oceanic floor, then goes back to the originator displaying the amount of time in ms(milliseconds) it took to send and receive. A server sets aside a process to complete the request, and it's no sweat off the back of a server that receives a few 'pings' at a time. But when a server is inundated with thousands of 'ping' requests from several different sources, all at once, then it becomes a little more difficult to handle the pings plus HTTP (Hyper Text Transfer Protocol) requests for a web page to load across the net, to some ones browser. Although this is an extreme case, net congestion can still become burdensome when a server has to handle several HTTP requests every second.

When you mix net congestion and connection speed together, you get a perfect recipe for creating digital mud. As a web designer, it's important that you develop a site with these factors in mind. This means not taking the fatal kiss of death that so many other web sites have taken by over stepping the conventional conservatism of design and development. To this end, one may say that the fatal kiss of death includes the usage of graphics that are extremely large in file size. If all your images on a single page combined equal 30 kilobytes or larger, the general rule of thumb states, 'They are too big'! Generally there is no rule as to how many graphics are considered too many graphics for a single web page, but keeping all this in mind when performing usability testing can save a lot of time and hassle down the road when it comes time to debugging. Another no-no is animation and over-emphasized, flashy designs that are equally poor in design taste, as well as slow. As a rule of thumb, animation should be limited to one or two locations per page, as any more than this can cause serious loading troubles for future users.

If you'd like to get an idea as to how large one of your pages is, compared to another professional web site, then here's a great remedy. Visit the page in question from your browser. From the browser's options across the top of the window, choose View, then scroll down to Source Code, or View Source. Highlight the entire script by dragging your mouse cursor across all the text (also called ascii) displayed (while holding down your left mouse button). Then press <CTRL>+C (by the way, <CTRL> means the CONTROL key on your keyboard) to copy the text to your cache. Then open a basic text editor and paste the text into it using <CTRL>+V. Save the file locally, in a place that's easy to find. Locate the file on your hard drive, then click on the file to highlight it. Click on the right mouse button while the file is highlighted, and choose Properties. Pay special attention to the 'size:' which is listed under the folder titled "general", and write this figure down somewhere. Then go back to the page on your browser (from an Internet connection to the server, don't view the local file as it resides in a directory on your computer, as this won't provide the same results). From the browser's options across the top of the window, choose View, then scroll down to Page Info. On the top part of the new window, you will see a series of hyperlinks for every image that appears in that page. You can get detailed information on each image simply by clicking on the available hyperlinks. You will get the exact image size in bytes (remember that 1,024 bytes makes 1 kilobytes), as the size displayed will not automatically convert. For instance, if the image is 74k, it will display as 75,776 bytes. Don't count duplicate images, as these are cached (stored) in memory from the initial page load. Then add up the total sum. This is a detailed approximation of your page's size. You can conduct this test for as many sites as you choose to view. If you aren't sure which page to compare, it's usually safe to use the default home page of every site you wish to research.

Another way to accomplish this, is to save each of the page images to your desktop by right clicking each image individually, and choosing 'save image as...", move the file to your computer, then get the file size from the file properties menu, similar to how I suggested you found the file size to the HTML script. This can get tricky if the home page has Macromedia FLASH running on it though, as you can't simply right click on it and download it. Instead, when you right click on it, FLASH will be displayed with no options listed. The file will already have been saved to a cached file on your computer. To find this file, go back to the Page Info window, find the hyperlink to the flash file, and copy the name of the file that is display in the properties portion of the lower window. Choose the tool on your computer that enables you to find files by filename, and type in the filename for the FLASH file. Once you have found this file, it should display the size of the file as well.

My favorite method though, is to simply open Microsoft Internet Explorer, go to the page you wish to check file sizes from, then from your browser, choose 'File', then 'Save As'. Make a new directory for this content, give the script a file name, and make sure that you've chosen the option 'Web Page, complete (*.htm, *.html)'. This will save a copy of their source code, along with all their images in a separate images directory. You can then visit your new directory and check out the file sizes of the images and source code!

Here's a list of web site sizes that might help (each is an approximation based on the steps used outlined above, and represents the total amount of space taken by both the scripts and images combined as well as the file size of the HTML):

http://www.ebay.com 96 KB combined, 47 KB for the HTML Script and 49 KB for the graphics.

http://www.amazon.com 93 KB combined, 53 KB for the HTML Script and 40 KB for the graphics

http://www.disney.com 60 KB combined, 23 KB for the HTML Script and 37 KB for the graphics (not counting the Flash file that gets loaded from their homepage).

http://www.earthlink.net 81 KB, 34 KB for the HTML Script and 47 KB for the graphics.

2.4.2 Cross Browser functionality

There was a time, fairly recent in fact, where a standardized WYSI-WYG format was the law of the land. WYSIWYG stands for What You See Is What You Get. This standard held true at the time, because there were only a couple different browsers to view the web site on, and it more or less looked the same on each browser.

It's a whole new ballgame now though, as there are multiple versions of browsers to check a web site against, not including platforms such as WebTV, laptop computer displays, or hand held PDA browsers for Palm Pilots, Windows CE systems or cellular phones.

One of the important aspects of web architecture is developing a site that is cross browser compatible. Just because it looks and functions terrific in Netscape, doesn't mean that it's going to be a big hit on Microsoft Internet Explorer, or WebTV, or higher vs. lower resolutions on different monitors. You obviously can't test for every type of configuration that's out there, but if you apply a couple of safety check features, and utilize a couple of pointers, chances are fair that your site will work universally.

You really only need to test against Netscape and Microsoft Internet Explorer, in order to appease the Internet Gods, and almost totally ensure that your web site will function and look the same when run on other browsers. Netscape Communicator and Microsoft Internet Explorer are two of the major browsers, and most widely distributed across the Internet. The only problem though is that many people still use outhouses instead of restrooms, and therefore utilize the most advanced sophistication in technology that money can afford (yesterdays technology, that is!). This means that many people haven't updated to the newest released version of the browser, and are using antiques that have been passed down the family lineage from father to son (keep in mind that browsers have only been around for a few years...). So although you may be testing against Netscape Communicator and Microsoft Internet Explorer, there is a good chance that many people will see something different, because they're using an older version of the browser. For instance, Netscape used to call their browser Netscape Navigator, so there was Navigator 1.0, 2.0 & 3.0 before they switched over to Netscape Communicator (which boasted a more user friendly interface, and upgrades that were not previously available.). Likewise, Microsoft has gone from Internet Explorer 1.0 to 5.0. If you are interested in knowing exactly how many people use one browser over another, here are some hot numbers for you.

I went to *http://www.statmarket.com* for some numbers related to Browser Trends in the market, and here's what they had to say...

On 4/3/1999, out of the total users on the Internet:

Microsoft Internet Explorer 4.x	52.16%
Netscape 4.x	25.85%
Microsoft Internet Explorer 5.x	8.31%
Microsoft Internet Explorer 3.x	5.92%
Netscape 3.x	4.86%
WebTV	1.86%
Microsoft Internet Explorer 0.x	0.78%
Netscape 5.x	0.15%
Netscape 2.x	0.01%

On 10/01/2001, out of the total users on the Internet

Microsoft Internet Explorer 6.x	9%
Microsoft Internet Explorer 5.x	71%
Microsoft Internet Explorer 4.x	5%
Netscape 4.x	5%

Note: The statistics for products not listed above are simply not included because I couldn't find accurate data to include for them.

They are still developing even newer versions as I write this, and chances are REALLY good, that by the time you read this, they will already have done away with the browser, and replaced it with a microchip that you inhale through your nose for a truly virtual reality web experience…Or maybe not…

Since you really only need to test against Netscape and Microsoft's web browsers, you should be aware of some of their differences. All browsers have a buffer space in the top left corner of the page. They differ, depending on which version of which browser, and for which computer (Macintosh or PC) you are using. Although you can turn off the buffer by using <body marginheight="0" marginwidth="0" topmargin="0" leftmargin="0">, it doesn't work in Netscape Navigator 3.x at all. The chrome also differs between browsers. What I mean by chrome, is the browser itself, such as the size of the buttons, the scrollbar, the information display bar at the bottom of the browser, etc…Each browser has a different height and width because there's no standard conformity between each browser's chrome. Because of the difference in pixel dimensions between browsers, what might fit on a single line in one browser, might take two lines in another to accomplish the same thing. This can be painful when your site web site look & feel is based on precision to detail.

When testing against other browsers, you should revert to a lower resolution. Usually it's much easier to develop and design a web site in a high resolution that gives you more room to maneuver, such as 1024 x 768 dpi (dots per inch), or even higher. However, the average user views a web site in a lower resolution of either 640 x 460 dpi or 800 x 600 dpi. Your web site should be built to fit in either of these two settings. As far as helping you decide which you should build for, 11 to 14 percent of current web users sees nothing larger than what fits within a 640-by-480 dpi display, while the larger audience goes to 800 x 600 dpi.

Laptop computers have a tendency to cut off the browser window just after the 'STOP' button at the top of the browser window (this button stops the page from loading, or requesting data from the HTTP server), which makes the 'STOP' button a good placement marker, for minimizing your browser window, so as to test how much of your site is viewable. It's alright to develop a site that scrolls vertically through information (even though you should generally develop a page that doesn't have to scroll too far down. Many people won't take the time to scroll down to find information.), but it's NOT alright to develop a web site where users must scroll horizontally across the screen to view the site. This is considered to be a big no-no in the Internet world.

There are many things to be aware of, so much so that I would have to write an entire book on usability to cover just a portion of the issues. Since someone else has already done this though, I guess I'll spare you the details. However, if you would like to learn more about usability issues, I would strongly suggest that you visit your local bookstore and purchase Designing Web Usability : The Practice of Simplicity by Jakob Nielsen (New Riders Publishing). If this sort of testing is of strong interest to you, then you might be even more interested to know that aside from the web designer positions available out there, there are also Usability Tester positions in the Dot Com industry. You spend a majority of your time cross checking a web site's performance, and handle issues that relate to incompatibility.

2.4.3 Building for WebTV

2.4.3.1 What is WebTV

If you haven't already guessed it, there are alternative means of viewing the Internet other than from a web browser on a personal computer. Take the standard television for instance, with the means of displaying reruns of game shows in low resolution, there simply had to be a way to truly exploit this advanced technology for the sake of non-computer users. That's how the web entertainment component module for the television came into existence. To come up with a name for this new Web TV device that would strike fear into the hearts of web designers all over the world, the founders hired a marketing firm for gazillions of dollars (a gazillion dollars is roughly the equivalent of three bags of rice and a tire pump in many third world nations such as Kansas.). After intensive study, evaluation, statistical analysis and countless Happy Hours, the marketing firm reached the pinnacle of their expertise and devised a name like no other. They gave it a name that represented the acme of revolutionary breakthrough in digital media entertainment, and the name of this Web TV device, was unleashed with unrivaled ingenious success as WebTV©®☺ ™. Much like a browser, WebTV can't connect to the Internet without a dialup connection from a major ISP. Also, you can't download files or applications to the WebTV unit from the Internet. It's strictly for viewing purposes only.

2.4.3.2 Designing Issues

WebTV uses a resolution of 560 x 384. You don't really need to develop for this narrow size though, because WebTV compresses the page to fit its width. Beware of cluttered layout design, though! Since WebTV crunch's everything together, your perfect web design might take a beating.

2.4.3.3 Using the WebTV Emulator

An emulator mimics exactly how the product's supposed to work without using the actually product to display the final result. In this case, you can download a free program that will simulate the WebTV browser on your PC or MAC so that you test your web page against this browser as well. I know you're thinking, "Jeesh! That's a lot of work, especially considering that a cost benefit analysis shows that most users won't even visit my site on WebTV!" But let me assure you that it's worth the extra effort. First off, there's your career to think about. You want Dot Com companies to know that you are a consciences web designer, and take every safety check and detail into professional consideration when building a site. Second off, there's the experience of using a new product, namely the WebTV Emulator. You should have experience with a large range of products in the development market, and heck it's free!

To download the WebTV emulator that simulates the WebTV browser, visit *http://developer.webtv.net/design/tools/viewer/*, then download and install the product.

2.4.4 Building for Wireless Cellular Phones

Few have ever made it through Los Angeles traffic and lived to tell about the horrific experiences to their grand children. Luckily though, I was trained in the ancient art of driving. I lived in Ohio for awhile, where dodging road-kill with only a split second to react after coming around a hairpin turn is considered the morning 'get to work' routine. In Los Angeles though, you ARE the road-kill. Los Angelinos drive 105 mph in neutral when there's bumper to bumper traffic (that is to say, all the time…), with one hand on the cellular phone, and the other hand on the car horn.

But now there's hope for a safer tomorrow. With the advances in wireless technology, people can now focus their undivided attention on surfing the Internet with their cellular phone from the convenience of their car, while in motion! Just think, if someone cuts you off on the freeway, you can pick up the cell phone, make an Internet connection, surf the web to your favorite free email service, then once the advertisements have finished loading, you can target that persons car using Global Positioning Satellites to track down their email address, then send an informative yet concerting email to that person (IE—"What's your malfunction, dork?!"), using the simple touch tone key pad on the cellular phone to type it out, and all while dodging bumper to bumper traffic at 105 mph with your other hand safely slamming the car horn.

2.4.4.1 What is WAP, WML, & WMLSCRIPT?

Since more and more people are actually receiving Internet services, such as web surfing, from the convenience of their cellular phones, there's a very good chance that at some point, it will be helpful for you (as the web designer) to know the concepts behind transitioning web site data to the smaller and less versatile WAP browser.

WAP stands for Wireless Application Protocol. Much like HTTP, the WAP enables information to flow via wireless connections. A WAP browser functions in the way Netscape Communicator or Microsoft Internet Explorer works, only scaled down. The features on a cellular phone web browser are minimal, as there's minimal space to work with.

WML is the scripting language used to create web pages for the WAP browser. WML stands for Wireless Markup Language. Just as HTML is an SGML (Standard Generalized Markup Language), so is WML. In fact, it's difficult in some ways to tell HTML and WML apart. This is good for development, as it should be easier to learn WML once you understand how to script HTML. However, WML has subtle changes. For instance, remember how HTML is an encapsulated scripting language where if you start a routine with <a href="http://www.blah!☺.com">, then you need to close it with </a>? With WML, it's a bit different. Instead of ending with </a>, you would instead end with <a/>. You don't have a selection of font types. You work in a deck (like a deck of cards), where each card represents a different page of your site. For navigation purposes, each card is labeled by a card ID that you create. Also, WML is a compiled language. You need a compiler to compress the script into the proper format, while HTML is an interpretive language that doesn't need to get compressed. Finally, remember how an HTML file end in the extension .htm or .html? Well, in the case of WML, the file ends with a .wml extension.

The WAP browser also utilizes WMLSCRIPT, which is very similar to JavaScript. It enables you add more powerful functionality to a very primitive SGML. I use the term primitive SGML because there is some heated debate between professionals as to whether WML should be the ultimate standard markup language for cellular phones. Because WML is more limited than HTML, and wireless technology is still in its infancy, many professionals want a stronger scripting language that can facilitate the expansion of the new emerging wireless market.

It's important that you keep up to date with the expansion of WAP. Many consider the wireless browsing market, the next great digital frontier, which puts you at the front of the line when Internet companies start researching ways to exploit its potential, and start looking to fill positions for web designers with knowledge of WAP, WML & WMLSCRIPT. How do you do that, you ask?! Well, for starters, have a book store party, and hang out in the computer isle, then read all you can get your hands on concerning WAP. Also, you can visit *http://www.nokia.com/* for user guides on WML, WMLSCRIPT, how WAP works, and the BIG incentive is that you can download for free, a working copy of their newest Nokia Cellular Phone emulator, which lets you develop WML files then compile and run them to test functionality and usability on a graphically rendered cellular phone (from your monitor) that looks and acts like the real thing. If you decide you want to actually produce live WML files for a cell phone though, you will need to be ready to pay for licensing the development tools.

2.4.4.2 Designing Issues for WAP Browsing

When you're designing for WAP Browsing, you need to keep aware of a couple issues. First off, you are working in monotone color (usually black and mercury green). This means that you'll be dealing with shades of gray. Images can be displayed on cellular phones, but it can only use bitmapped images that end in the .bmp extension. Also, you are working in a much more confining space. Instead of a leisurely 800 x 600 resolution, you'll probably be working in an environment that's closer to 100 x 100 or smaller! There's no standard resolution for a cellular phone display, so I'm giving you a generalization here. Look for standardization to probably occur within our lifetime however. It's also a good idea to keep Adobe Photoshop in mind. In this case, you can download the Nokia Cellular Phone emulator from their web site, then install and run the program. Once you see the graphically rendered Nokia Cellular phone on your computer monitor, you can press the PrtScn button on your keyboard to make a screen capture. Paste the screen capture into Photoshop, then you can mockup screenshots for WML as well. Remember, you'll want to have an impressive portfolio of rendered screenshots when you go to your Internet company interviews, so you'll want to be collecting stuff like this!

2.4.5 Building for Palm Pilots

First there were pocket protectors, then there were large graphing calculators sticking out of people's pockets. After a while the pocket book was developed (complete with a smaller calculator), followed by the Day Planners and the Electronic Organizers. Then, just when you thought there couldn't possibly be another revolutionizing breakthrough in technology, the wireless handheld Palm Pilot was invented.

2.4.5.1 What is a Palm Pilot, and Do I need a Pilots License to Operate It?

Since the company Palm is now a publicly traded Corporation and enjoys 78.4% of the handheld market (IDC, 1999), it's probably a good idea to bring them into the picture. A Palm Pilot is a really sophisticated pocket protector, developed to be the ultimate electronic day planner (with the ability to surf the Internet, check email, and transmit data from your computer to the handheld device), which competes against Microsoft Windows CE (a scaled down but equally expensive color version of Windows Operating System) and other wireless handheld manufacturers such as Blackberry, Handspring, and Hewlett Packard among others. In case you actually paid attention to the headline for this segment, the answer is YES! You REALLY DO need a pilot's license to operate these handheld devices, but not just ANY pilot's license sold in stores. You can only get these authentic hand scripted aluminum plated licenses by sending 200 equal monthly installments of $99.99 to...Actually, No. The answer is no, you really don't need a license of any kind to operate these handheld devices. Unless you REALLY want a one of a kind, authentic, personally signed license, in which case, send your CASH ONLY payments to...

2.4.5.2 PALM SDK

Although you can't actually surf the web on a Palm handheld device yet, you can still get vital information from the Internet via their 'web clipping' technology where Palm has partnered with several online sites to offer specific features via the Internet such as stock quotes, and movie show times, etc...Pretty soon though, browsing the web might just be a standard function of the handheld devices, including the Palm Pilot, therefore you might as well know a little something about developing for it.

The Palm displays a resolution of 160 x 160 (future Palm screen sizes may differ). This is similar to a cellular phone where your working space is limited. Many of the current Palm Pilots are monotone in color, and utilize only a grayscale color palette, but they are in the process of developing newer palm pilots that use 8-bit (216 web safe) colors and higher. In order to develop for the Palm, you should use the latest version of the PALM SDK, which is their patented Software Developer Kit. The programming language for Palm is pretty darned close to C++, which means it's NOTHING like HTML. Given time though, the handheld market will more than likely include browser support that will require a web designer's expertise. If you are interested in developing for the Palm Pilot though, visit **www.palm.com** then click on Development Zone. You will find vast developer resources including their PALM SDK and programming tutorials, including information on CodeWarrior, which is an Interactive Developer Environment (IDE) from 3Com Corporation, and is also the most widely used handheld development tool around.

2.5 Putting the Structure Together

The idea situation of course, would have been to have Mr. Bubba (executive representative of Billy Joe's Tuna Taco Stand) hand you a check for the amount necessary in hiring an outsourced consultant that could hassle over the actual building phase of your new home! However, for purposes of this tutorial, and because you developed the ultimate hypothetical web presence for Mr. Billy Joe and his sidekick Mr. Bubba, they've agreed to substitute your billing rate totaling hundreds of thousands of dollars in exchange for 1,000,000 hypothetical shares of company stock in the all new pre-IPO BillyJoe'sTunaTacoStande.com (look at that, you're on your way to becoming a millionaire already, and that's just hypothetically speaking!). Just think of your actual job market potential as a seasoned web designer in the pre-IPO Dot Com marketplace! But you're not quite there yet, because you still have to…

2.5.1 Choose Your Tools Wisely

I know you're now quivering with delight at the thought of cashing in those shares that Mr. Billy Joe so generously and hypothetically gave you. Heck, if it were me, I'd be thinking of all the rewarding ways of spending those hard earned stock options. In fact, I'd probably purchase a state-of-the-art ant farm, with auto temperature adjuster and robotic feeding claw (it puts shivers down my spine just thinking about the possibilities!), but right now it's time to focus on the all-important issue of development. You're finally at that stage where it's time to decide whether your site is going to be more content heavy, full of multimedia thrills, and structured to offer the best in bleeding edge technology, or whether it's going to take a more conservative approach and stick to traditional text and images.

It really depends on what you will be providing to your audience though, and what kind of mood you want to get people in. In a lot of ways, you should consider yourself a writer/director/producer...You have to set an environment on a stage that draws the users total attention. No, big blinking banners aren't the answer. In fact, major surveys have concluded that people get irritated by ANYTHING that flashes or blinks on the Internet. This means that you will want to choose the tools that will help you accomplish the difficult task of setting the mood. For instance, if you run a classical music retail shop on the net, you could use splashy graphics, and smooth anti-aliased Macromedia Flash animations creating a more spunky tone for your site, or you could use a more classy approach, using boring old standard text and simple images to provoke a more classical mood. Either way, you're going to attract audiences to your site, so the question really boils down to what kind of audience you really want to attract.

You also need to keep in mind what it takes to keep someone on a website for as long as possible. This is considered the 'click through rate', and it is fairly important. Generally, a user's click through rate averages 3 to 4 page views per visit, meaning that they are literally visiting three to four different pages on a web site. In other words, the person didn't get immediately bored, and you found some smart way to present enough information to the user so that they wanted to click deeper into your site for further information. You've got to remember that the Internet was invented specifically to tailor information browsing via hyperlinks. The best way to utilize this to your advantage, is to offer tantalizing information that gives just enough to draw users attention, and just enough more that causes them to want to click on the hyperlink transporting them deeper into the recessive bowels of your web site. Don't ever give ALL your information away on the first page.

The downside to this information approach is that if your site uses multimedia more extensively, then your users will experience longer delays in receiving data, and won't bother to stay on your site long enough to enjoy it. Most people will wait for up to 15 seconds before they jump ship and swim to more inviting shores. But don't get too comfortable with this number, because it's a variable based on several factors that keep getting upgraded, including delay constraints caused by server capacity, network issues, net congestion, browser display, image decompression, and line noise among others.

2.5.2 The Directory Structure

One of the most important decisions you'll make as a web designer has to do with data repository management. Data repository management is when you have several files that have to be organized in an easy to find manner. In many ways, you'll become a net librarian whose key concern is to efficiently organize files in a repository, or dumping bin (usually a folder specifically set aside as a dumping ground for your sub directories and files). When you're setting up your very first web site, and most other basic web sites, you'll find that data management is fairly easy. Essentially you dump all your HTML files and image files into a single directory (in many ways, this is like throwing all your clothes on the floor instead of hanging them up in the closet). A basic web site generally consists of four to five HTML files (making up the home page and a couple other pages), and some images to spice up your site. When you get into the big league of web development though, you'll find that the number of files needed to run a web site grow exponentially! When you're working with an Internet company, and you need to make a simple text change to a specific HTML template, you'll find it can get pretty aggravating when you must spend countless hours scouring through fifty or more files when they're not organized to begin with.

It's usually a good idea to practice good storage methods early on, as this will help fine tune your ability to create a robust and scalable hierarchy on a larger scale when you move into the professional realm.

Sketching out an order for your file structure can assist you in establishing a directory tree. I use the word 'tree' because you usually start off on the main directory (the trunk of your tree), and stem out your sub directories (branches) to create mini dumping grounds depending on how you choose to organize your files. One method is to have your trunk consist of main template files (home page, second and third page, etc...), then create a sub directory for your images. Since the home page file is your flagship file, it must reside in the main directory under most circumstances. This is mostly because servers aren't programmed to search in sub directories for the default file that initially loads a web site. Remember that when a web site loads, it always starts with your home page file, which is usually named either index.htm or index.html. Most Internet companies use a more industrial approach to maintaining the directory structure. This is done for a number of reasons. One of which is that if you spend several days making changes to some HTML files, then someone else in the company works on the same files, they might overwrite your changes since they would have written over an earlier version of the page, excluding any work you might have painstakingly labored over. Another issue is developing for a 'live site'. A live site represents the finished product. Internet companies usually have several projects being worked on simultaneously, but once a project is completed, it still has to be signed off and run through QA (Quality Assurance) for bugs and usability testing before it can be added to the 'live site'. Because of these problems, Internet companies utilize a CVS system for managing data on a larger scale. CVS stands for Concurrent Versions System, and as a version control system that allows you to keep old versions of files as backup, and logs who made changes to what, when and why. CVS enables you to set up a branch for specific projects, wherein you can make changes to duplicates of original files, view the changes, then merge the duplicates over the original files (otherwise known as merging the branch to the trunk) if all is well. CVS doesn't actual duplicate the files, but it 'Tags' them as different versions. Plus, everyone works in their own playpen, or sandbox, so that if someone else needs to work on the same project, and in the same CVS branch as you, they have a lesser chance of overwriting your files. If they accidentally commit their changes over your own, you can easily go back to an earlier 'Tagged' version of the files to get lost changes back again.

2.5.3 Building the Skeleton

Remember that a web site is indefinitely in the construction phase. It's like building the perfect house. Even though it's quite perfect, it's never perfectly livable without some additional miner touchup details, such as…oh, say…furniture. Then the furniture is never quite perfect on it's own without being moved a million times.

So you are now at the bare bones stage. This is the phase where you don't need to focus on adding the furniture, but instead you just need to worry about having four solid walls and a ceiling.

In fact, by now you've got several mockups and specifications that go over the overall concept of the site, including what your site will accomplish, how it will accomplish it, what the general layout will be like, and some rough sketches covering design interface and layout. Now you should setup the necessary HTML templates to fulfill the most basic of design. Since your site is always in the construction phase, don't think that your web pages have to be absolutely perfect right off the bat. Piano teachers will instruct you to keep playing straight through the musical piece even if you've turned Mozart into a rougher sounding Metallica, and typing instructors will give you timed drills where mistakes will be made, but you simply must keep typing as it's just not time efficient to correct your mistakes during the drill. The same goes for the web site. Effective time management can be crucial to launching a web site on a tight schedule. Especially for a Dot Com company that must show quick results to those that have invested lots of Angel, Seed or Venture Capital funding. So learn early to use your time efficiently when developing web sites. Build a basic structure that you can go back to later for detail work. Make sure you reach your objectives off the bat for functionality though. After all, no sense in building four walls and laying down a carpet when you've fudged on the roof, and left gapping holes that will do you no good during a major rain storm.

2.6 The Finishing Details

Have you ever walked through a brand new home in a newly developed community? The house usually looks like a lavish mansion on the outside, but the minute you step foot inside, it's like being welcomed into a very expensive yet empty and hallow warehouse lacking everything from carpet and tile to toilets and doors. It's an utter mess. Yet, it retains it's external visual appeal as a respectable abode. In many ways, your newly built web site has the likeness of this example. After all, it looks like a web site overall, yet it will probably initially lack many of the interior luxuries that make it a completed product.

2.6.1 Branding and Logo Treatment

Branding is an important term when dealing with a web site. Branding is a way of advertising the web site to your users so it becomes a household name (Take for example these household names: Bill, Brenda, Timmy and http://www.stephanie-gone_Digital!.com). Your ultimate goal is not only to draw attention to your site, but also to keep them on your site for as long as possible, and then to have them come back again and again. Merchandising and positioning can be a powerful ally when trying to win user appeal. Take for instance *http://www.pets.com*. It's easy to know from the domain name that this site has to do with pets. However, what's going to influence your decision to use their site instead of the countless other sites that cater to the same market? For *http://www.pets.com*, they've created a sock puppet to splash up their image. This added to an upbeat interface design make for a strongly branded model with an even stronger sense of self and direction. Wishy-washy doesn't go over very well on the internet. And considering that strongly impacting sites have made the net a more competitive place to reside, it's important that you develop around a central theme and maintain that mantra throughout all your pages. Tone, Consistency and User-Friendly are a few of the terms that seem to work well with audiences on the World Wide Web.

One way to accomplish tone is to look at competitors and see what they're doing. Another way is to focus on your original goals. What kind of audience are you looking to reach, and what do you have to offer? What makes your site any more qualified than the next? If you are with a Dot Com company, chances are good that you might get to work with an out-sourced marketing and media firm to hash out a design model for your site. While some sites stick to mascots such as characters like lovable dirty socks with eyeballs, others use logo treatment to their benefit. Some have a firm belief that consistency is the key to impacting design, after all, if you see their exact same logo on page after page, doesn't that eventually become an anchor in a users mind and complete an overall strong sense of design? For instance, fill in the blanks below and see what I mean.

Less filling, tastes _____.

Nike. Just ____ ____.

Chances are very good that you can guess with certainty what words go in those blank spots (the answers are 'Less filling, tastes great' and 'Nike. Just Do It.'), which makes them an embedded anchor. However, consistency isn't the essential key to strong design, although it is a piece of the puzzle. Tone is closely related to identity. And the term 'identity' can be best translated into a set of characteristics whereby a thing is recognizable. So although consistency in placement and images can back up or fortify an identity in rich media, it's ultimately how you express your position and goals through your media rich channel that will set the tone. How's that for guru prophetic advice!

Logo treatment will give you a chance to work closely with Adobe Photoshop and Illustrator. If you've decided on a name for your web site, or have a company name that you'd like to transition to the web, then logo treatment will add the flare that will differentiate your site from the masses. First off, what's in a name? Well, considering that the domain name 'business.com' sold for over seven million dollars, I'd have to say quite a bit. It's not enough to have a good name though. After all, if you have a killer name such as toemunchemcurdletea&corporated, it's not going to be enough when your name in all its glory is only displayed as text on your web site. So get creative! Perhaps a bolt of electricity ripping through your name, cutting it in half, leaving sparks and a slight cast shadow will do the trick. Or perhaps, it's a simple yet sharp outline.

Although I can't instruct you on what to choose for your logo, just be aware that web based logos and branding are relevant.

2.6.2 The Layout and Design

When you're focusing on the layout and design of your site, one of the things you'll want to consider is eye placement and movement. Does your site read easily from top to bottom or from left to right? Do all the elements align with good use of placement? You need to imagine that there's an invisible gridline that exists in cyberspace. You can also imagine that there are lots of cute little furry creatures carrying all your data from the browser to the server, or not. But the point is, your formatting should be consistent. If some of your text is justified to the left, does the rest of your content also align to fit the page properly? Spend some time on other web sites, and pay close attention to how their interface is laid out. You'll find that there are many professionals in the field that utilize the imaginary grid. You'll also find that many of them REALLY DO believe that there are cute little furry creatures in cyberspace that carry your data from the browser to the server. Sometimes you might design web sites in a higher resolution, but it's a good idea to minimize your browser to about 640 x 480 pixels every once in a while to view your progress, as this is the standard size that people use to view web pages (if you're not sure how to do this accurately, simply change the resolution on your desktop to 640 x 480, then fully expand your browser). You might be very surprised to find that where you thought your logo and navigation bar were the absolute first things seen by users to your site, that in fact your users that visit your site in 640 x 480 are only seeing the top of your logo, and a small portion of your navigation bar. By the way, it's interesting to note that there was a time many moons ago when navigation bars were generally to the left and ran down the length of the page. However, by today's standards, the navigation bar generally runs across the top, and along the width of the page. Although there are no definite rules you need to abide by when determining placement and positioning of site content, just be aware that there is a general way of placing stuff on a site, and people generally feel most comfortable with what they already know.

Design emphasis is equally important. I've been on websites where experimental visual queues were used in place of what would otherwise have been standard text. For instance, the site displayed no text. It only showed a graphical nose with an arrow pointing to the nostrils and a product of some kind. I suspect their intention was for me to smell their product by clicking on animated bubbles that would drip from the nostrils, burst and then leak plentiful juices across my screen. It only succeeded in making me nauseous. I've been on sites that used such strongly worded terminology, that I simply got lost just by trying to use their search feature! Instead of simple terms such as 'search' or 'find', they used scary terms such as 'Central Data Stationary Search' or 'Referential Deferral Help Desk Scan Bot Utility'. Essentially what they failed to accomplish was standard English.

Keep in mind that just because you're using an electronic medium for providing digital information to your users, that you don't have to present your information as though it's coming from the heart and mind of a computer console. It simply doesn't register through my CPU to default null where no character = 0......um, anyways...What Im trying to say is that you should give your site some personality and flavor, but keep it simple and friendly. If you would like to study further information on media rich design concepts and learn from the pros with experience, then I suggest that you visit your local bookstore again, and purchase 'Designing Business—Multiple Media, Multiple Disciplines' by Clement Mok (Adobe Press, 1996). Another great book that focuses fully on front-end technologies and acts as an excellent reference for HTML and overall web design is 'Web Design in a Nutshell' by Jennifer Niederst (O'Reilly & Associates).

2.6.3 Choosing a Color Scheme

Green goes great with blue. But then, blue goes great with yellow. And yellow does wonders with red. However red can look so sleek when used with black. So, if all these colors go so well together, what's the problem? The problem is that there are too many colors being discussed. Many a web designer would cringe at the thought of having to develop a site that used ALL those colors at once. After all, this isn't exactly like Joseph and the Amazing Technicolor Dreamcoat, where it's groovy to use okra and peach and violet and red and crimson and rose and olive and mauve and pink and black and white and orange and blue! (although I didn't say them in the same order as the famous play, since that would probably get me into a little bit of trouble, which is another way of becoming famous, but we won't go there…). But am I PAINT-ING my picture clearly enough for you? (no pun intended…). Simply put, you should choose a color palette with 2 to 4 main colors on your site, then use darker and lighter shades from your chosen color palette. This way your site doesn't take a more comical circus approach, unless of course that was your goal and intention to begin with. It might sound a bit conservative to use this approach, but what it comes down to is over-all look and feel, which leads me to…

2.6.4 The Overall Look and Feel

When you work on a web site with other designers, you might find yourself talking the artsy mojo. Now, for newer web designers from other professions, this may take some getting use to, but in a lot of ways, you've got to remember that web designing is not only a field of its own with a language and environment that suites the designers best, but also a cre-ative role that encourages expressing thoughts out of the corporate box. For instance, Let's look at a VERY brief conversation between Surje, a web designer and Bob, a mechanical engineer:

Surje: I really feel as though the essence of the site is driving me on an emotional level.

Bob: Huh?

Surje: Well, I mean just look at the imagery and content development. It's as if a riveting wind of color is splashing hues of freshness before my eyes. Alluring them if you will, to the central focus of the page.

Bob: But there's only a single hyperlink in the middle of the page...

Surje: Yes. In fact, YES! It's like an inner force is guiding my strength and yielding a tempting option to click through to the next segmented graphical construct.

Bob: It's ONLY a link!

Of course, this is an exaggerated example. In reality as a web designer, you will more than likely be expected to know the web-centric terminology and use it in a concise and professional manner. After all, you will essentially be the front-end site contact for the company. This being the case, you will more than likely have to discuss problems, issues and enhancements in an intelligible manner with other divisions within the company. However, when Look and Feel issues come into play, it's important that you convey your feelings as an artist for how the structure is presented.

You are probably wondering what kind of issues there are when dealing with Look and Feel. Basically, you take a web site, and analyze it on a page by page basis. You make sure that eye movement is choreographed so that the user can maintain steady and constant visualized flow from the top of the page to the bottom of the page, or from the left of the page to the right of the page. For instance, if you center align a large font sized title at the top of the page, is it more aesthetically appealing to the eye to center align the content text underneath the title? Where do the images go in relation to the text? And what is an appropriate size for the images when sharing the same space with smaller font sized text? The answer to this is proportional integrity. What portion of the site should draw the users attention first? Probably not the loud and obnoxious blinking banner advertisement at the top of the page. Attention could first go to the title of the content, then to the content it relates to, or first to the navigation bar of the page, then to where the user is in relation to the rest of the site, then to the images, and finally to the title and content. The point is, you should be careful not to just throw a bunch of elements on a web page, without making sure they align correctly to your imaginary grid, are aesthetically appealing and utilize good proportional integrity. If you feel this type of work is right up your alley, then you're not alone. There are several people that work professionally as User Interface (UI) Designers. A UI Designer is assigned the task of creating and working with Photoshop mockups of page layouts, then writing the page to code in HTML, and finally making sure that the page maintains it's Look and Feel universally across different browsers, resolutions, and computer systems. In fact, for terrific tutorials on Interface Design, Look and Feel, and usability issues, I strongly suggest that you read Designing Web Usability by Jakob Nielsen (New Riders, 2000). I also suggest that you start spending more time with web designers named Surje.

2.7 I've Built the Web Site, Now What?

Give yourself a nice pat on the back. You've just gone through the rigors and trials of developing a web site from scratch. I know you're thinking this must be the perfect time to close this guide and celebrate by visiting your neighbors and friends, so that they can connect to the Internet and check out your terrific new site, but hold your horses for just a second. The only way you could visit your newly built site at this stage, would have been by developing the site on ***http://www.homestead.com***, or other Internet based web site builder that conveniently gives you quick and efficient tools for site enhancement (I don't recommend that as a new web designer you use any web based HTML tools for layout or other, as they detract from your ability to experience and learn the essentials of HTML scripting). If you built your site another way, such as a WYSIWYG (What You See Is What You Get) HTML editor, it usually comes equipped with the ability to transfer your files to the server that will house your site. If however you constructed your site using the steps I've outlined in the course of this tutorial, then you will find that you haven't yet gotten to the major step of transferring your files to the Internet.

2.7.1 The FTP Protocol

So you've got this groovy site, and it's all built to code, but the snag now is actually moving the finished product from your hard drive (local client-side terminal) to the server that will push your site to the WWW (Whole Wide World—mind you, that's not what WWW REALLY stands for...Refer to the Introduction of this guide for a refresh!). In a lot of ways, it's like finally finishing your mansion, that you built it in a huge parking lot, and finally need to move the whole house to the new property. In the case of a big house, you could probably have trucks haul it for you (a more manageable and economic approach would be to rent a U-Haul, and just move the pieces yourself, but I don't advise this approach).

When you initially created the web site, you were only viewing it from your local hard drive. This was accomplished by opening the browser, without making a dialup connection to the Internet, then choosing Open File from the menu bar at the top of the browser, and choosing the HTML file you wished to viewed. This also meant that others couldn't view your web site unless you physically moved the files that made up your site from your hard drive to theirs. They couldn't actually see your web site from the Internet until you FTP'd all the web site files to the server. Only then could someone on another computer, type in your URL, and see the finished product.

2.7.2 Binary Vs. Ascii

The FTP Protocol is analogous to the truck that will haul your house from one place to another. FTP stands for File Transfer Protocol, and enables you to swiftly and quickly move your files from your local hard drive to the server. I recommend the FTP application called WSFTP for this process, as you can download a free trial version from *http://www.wsftp.com*. When you FTP files from one place to another, it's important to mention which method of transfer is best for ascii (any text based code) vs. images and multimedia files. Ascii files are best transferred in ascii mode (see the neat relation?), while images and multimedia files should transfer in binary mode. If you transfer ascii text (such as an HTML template like myfile.htm) in binary mode, you'll end up with strange escape characters (something like this, '^M') trailing every line in your code. This can cause problems. Equally problematic are images that are transferred in ascii mode. They simply won't work right, if at all once they are uploaded.

2.7.3 How does this help me get that pre-IPO Dot Com job?!

It's obvious that you don't need to follow the steps outlined in this guide to create a web site, but if you want to create a knockout web site that herds in the users every time, then it's best you focus your energy into following these guidebook steps as well as reading through the materials I've suggested. Everything I've covered (which is actually a small portion of the overall process, but at least the most necessary of steps…) is used in the professional world of web design and development. In fact, as a seasoned Interface Developer, I can tell you that it impresses the heck out of Creative Directors when you mention how you've read and applied the works of Jakob Nielson (who is one of the worlds leading web usability experts).

3. Getting Lots of Experience

3.1 Building a Portfolio

For those of us that never had to worry about setting up a portfolio in our previous professional careers, it's probably a good idea that we discuss the intricacies of portfolio building. I'm positive that the 'portfolio' was originally brought about to accommodate prehistoric man at the dawn of creation. This would explain to struggling archaeologists why caves contained ancient piles of skulls and bones. While scientific reason would lead the most brilliant to believe it meant there was a huge party going on one night when a flash stampede of wooly mammoths trampled them all to death, I on the other hand have a different opinion. I'm sure that early man collected skulls and bones, washed, waxed and polished them, then kept them in a portfolio as a means of securing good employment with benefits at such prestigious early hotspots as Gog's Ugh Inc. or Mug Glog Corp. If they had a REALLY good portfolio, there was even the chance of getting into IBM. Later the Latin people came up with a Latin term called 'portare' meaning 'to carry'. Combined with the Latin term 'folio' meaning 'leaf sheet', this formed a very powerful combination indeed, except portar-folio didn't have the same aerodynamic flow, so it was shortened to portfolio. After several stress tests, it was accepted by the general population to mean 'way of carrying polished skulls and bones'.

3.1.1 Getting Exposure to the Net

A lot of web designers like to critique others work. Since you are now a web designer yourself, it's time you start getting into the habit of applying critical thought to each and every web site you visit. In addition, you should start looking at diversifying yourself by visiting as many web sites as possible. Look at basic home pages built by other people, professional corporate web sites, government based web sites, expand your horizons by visiting several competing sites within different industries. The reason I suggest this, is because there is always someone with more experience than you, and then always someone with more experience with them. Your goal should be to visit, study and identify what works on the net and what doesn't. For instance, does the color palette work? How are they formatting their layout? Do they use a good approach to navigation? You should mentally create a 'To Do' checklist in your head, so that you end up using a systematic approach to breaking down a site during your critique. Does their HTML Source Code look clean? Would you have done anything different? Was there anything that stood out to you about their site that you liked? Is it something you could see yourself applying to web sites?

It's extremely important that you know what the competition looks like out there. It's also good that you are familiar with what tools are being used to accommodate the web site content. For instance, are designers using Macromedia for stunning visual effects, and do they work? Do they use JavaScript, and is it effective? The more able you are to critically distinguish between a well developed web site and a poorly developed site, the better your ability will be to create award quality and highly acclaimed design on the Internet that will reap the praise of employers when you seek professional employment.

3.1.2 Why a Web Portfolio?

A web portfolio is your way of impressing the socks off your interviewer when you seek professional employment. It's often just as effective to have a stunning portfolio of your best work, as it is to simply list URL's for employers to view. All too often, an employer will request to see samples of your work. The difference is when you refer them to a URL, you usually don't get to discuss your strengths and why you chose certain design elements. The GREAT thing about having your best works available in a portfolio, is that you can layout the before and after stages of your evolving design. For instance, as you gain experience by designing a site, you will find that your site is always under construction. In fact, EVERY site is always under construction! Web sites are always experiencing constant evolving change. Sometimes the change is slight, such as an added image or reformatted text, or sometimes major, where the entire page gets redesigned. Since you as a web designer will be caught up in this evolution process with the content you develop, it's important that you make screen shots of every web page you create. Add these screen shots to your portfolio, and have them handy at your interview because they are an invaluable tool for showing the before and after of your site evolution. Interviewers love seeing visual aids, especially when they give you a chance to point out why you chose certain aesthetic elements in your content.

3.1.3 Kinkos and Color Prints

Now that we've established the importance of maintaining a screen shot based portfolio of your web work, it's time to discuss what your portfolio is physically made up of. For instance, some people choose to simply keep their portfolio digital, and on mediums such as CD-ROM, ZIP disks (capable of storing 100 MB of information), or uploaded to the server where their personal web site resides so it's available for viewing anytime by anyone with the URL and an Internet connection.

I think it's important to have backups available using these previously mentioned mediums, but I also think you should always have your work available in the form of color prints, that can placed on a table top and handed to the interviewers (they love tangible eye candy). Besides, it's much easier to place color prints side by side for comparisons when discussing the before and after of your site evolution.

So with this in mind, where and how do you make these color prints, and where do you keep them? The best solution is to spend a ton of money on an expensive color laser printer and glossy paper to print your materials at your convenience. However with most people, money is an issue. If you are unable to purchase a color laser printer and glossy paper, then I suggest you find your local Kinkos or other printing shop, and be prepared to make several visits to their facility. They usually have the equipment necessary in creating high quality prints of your work. All you have to do is bring the prints in a standard file format such as .jpg or .gif and on a disk that can be read by their equipment (for instance, you might have a great Jazz Drive disk that stores all your screen shots on, but you may find that your local printing facility doesn't have a Jazz Drive to transfer the files to their equipment).

The best place to keep these prints is actually up to you. I feel comfortable interviewing with a standard manila folder full of my prints. However, you may feel more comfortable with a zipper based portfolio case, which can be purchased in most major art stores. It really doesn't matter, so long as you use a case that will protect your work from the three evil forces of nature.

1. Little kids with Peanut Butter and Jelly sandwiches

2. Dogs with slimy wet noses and foaming mouths

3. Interviewers with Smudgy fingers (usually from Doritos, Pepsi, and Twinkies!)

3.1.4 What to Add and What to Flush

You will probably get the urge to add every little thing to your portfolio. It's only natural. Especially when you spent hours of painful manual labor creating the content on each web page. But let me tell you in advance that too many prints of previous work can do more damage than good. First off, your interviewer will suffer from information overload, and secondly, chances are greater that you'll add pages that don't represent your absolute best in design or development.

It's usually sufficient to have between three to four sets of before & after screen shots per each web site you've developed (this also goes for web sites in which you were a member of a web development team). It's true that you want to sell yourself to the employer, but it's also true that you should want to sell your 'best' self to the employer. So spend some time before each interview deciding on which pages you'd like to focus on, and give considerable thought to what aspects of the page design and development you will discuss. It's important that you are able to present each page to the interviewer with a history as to the importance of the page in relation to the site, and an active description as to how a user would have gotten to the page, what the page is for, and then why you chose certain design elements (taking specific issues into account, such as layout, look & feel, color, positioning, font type and size, formatting, size and width constraints, and whatever else you may feel inspired to discuss that's relevant and important).

3.2 Finding New Places to Build

It's important that you practice your newly gained skills. The great thing about web development is that you can practice adding content to web pages while adding content to your resume as well. Two great things will abound from this win/win situation. First off, practice makes permanent. This means that the more you apply your new skills, the better you will become at expert site design. Secondly, the best way to practice is to offer your services initially for either an extremely reduced price or free. This will allow you to draw a strong customer base thus adding strong experience to your resume, and will also give you the ability to create several web pages that can be used in your portfolio.

3.2.1 Building a Finding Pool

You should either purchase a white board and dry erase markers, or have sketch paper readily handy (if you have children terrorizing your house, like myself, then I strongly recommend stealing their crayons and line paper as this is much more convenient and economical). I offer this sound advice because it will give you the opportunity to chart out which clients are 'in the zone'. In this case, you should segregate your board or sheet into three distinct areas, and title them as follows:

1. Finding Pool
2. In Development Pool
3. Work Complete Pool

As you go out to find new potential clients, you would list the potentials in your 'Finding Pool'. Once you've received the sign-off to create award winning content for your established client, you would move them over to the 'In Development Pool'. Finally, once all the work is complete, and the client is satisfied with the work, you should move them to the 'Work Complete Pool'.

This process enables you to juggle several projects while visualizing their progress on different levels. It's true that you could probably do this in your head, but consider it good working exercise, since many web development teams in the professional realm use white boards and sketch pads to visualize their progress on content projects.

3.2.2 Utilizing Participant Observation

I find it interesting that Sociology and Sosisi are not related in anyway, shape, or form. Sosisi is a Samoan term for Sausage. Sociology is the intricate science of studying the cultures of people like Samoans who create terms like Sosisi. Sociologists spend a majority of their time swallowing exotic Mangrove worms in an attempt to fit in with the locals (although the locals actually prefer Big Macs and Fries), and justifying their hiatus fieldtrips to such terrifying and exotic places such as Club Med Australia by establishing new scientific terminology. For instance–

University Board: How was your trip to the exotic and terrifying outback of Australia?

Sociologist: Gee, it was great. I got a swell tan.

University Board: Considering that your trip cost our school nearly $60,000 did you learn anything new?

Sociologist: Ahem (scratching the head)…Um…Yes, uh…I believe I'm on to something big. Major, in fact……(long pause).

University Board: Well?

Sociologist: Yes…Well…(longer pause) . Utilizing participant observation (new scientific term), I found that the norms (new scientific term) were socially stratified (new scientific term) and in direct proportion to the interactionism (new scientific term) of the upwardly mobile (new scientific term)…

University Board: Wonderful. We'd like to send you to Sweden now.

Sociologist: Really?!

Which brings me to the point I wanted to make. Sociology coined the term 'Participant Observation', which is a form of observation where researchers participate to some extent in the lives of those being studied.

Participant Observation is important for web designers in training. By utilizing this sociological function, a web designer can study the web environment, learn the culture and language, and become a member of the elite and highly exotic group of professional web designers who are scattered across the world.

When studying other web designers, focus should be given to the process by which work is achieved. You will probably find that there are several ways to achieve a basic goal of completing the product, either because the production differs or because the assignments of the designers differ. You're probably thinking, 'What great advice, Aaron. How the heck do you expect me to find web designers in the first place?! Hmm...Although you DID mention that they're exotic. Does that mean I should be looking in my garden?!'. Okay, so it's true that web designers hide in the wall cracks and only come out when tempted by food, but there's an easier way to do this. First off, wherever you are currently working, there's bound to be a website, and someone has to maintain it, so find out who, and introduce yourself. Or, you can hold off until you have the chance to interview with companies for this position, where you can ask several detailed questions about their production process, and possibly see some web designers in action. Another way is to call around, and explain that you are a student who's anxious to learn more about their web team. Just make sure that you bring a bag of chips to lure them out of the walls.

3.2.3 Where to Look for Clients

There are many ways to establish a finding pool. Remember that your finding pool is a simple list of potential clients. Everyone you talk to is a potential client, from your next door neighbor to your local store clerk. You should get a feel for discussing web site issues with people by approaching them in casual conversation, then asking whether they currently have a web site of their own, or have ever thought of having a web site. You will be amazed at the level of perception you receive to such a topic. Many people feel left behind in this fast moving digital revolution, and would sincerely love to get up to speed, except they feel as though they are so far behind in understanding that they simply will never catch up, and therefore should not bother. However if you offer your services to either teaching them how to get up to speed, or offer to build them a free web site (don't go for profit until you've setup several web sites and have credentials behind you), that will usually spark their interest. Some people might not have an immediate use for a web site without a little push, which gives you a great chance to offer examples as to how a web site might benefit them. You are not only selling your services and yourself to your potential clients, but you are reinforcing your working knowledge of web development through iteration and memory recall. Every person that looks even slightly interested should be added to your finding pool.

Just remember to look your best before interviewing, even at the volunteer level. Professionalism is everything. Even though the dress code in the industry is thongs, shorts and Hawaiian shirts, you have to get in the front door first. This means setting a terrific first impression. And because you only get one chance at making a first impression, you need to be at your very best. Wear appropriate business attire, such as slacks, button down and tie, or if you are a bit more feminine, a nice dress or blouse would be suitable. Go in with a smile of confidence. Show determination through your movements and actions. Always maintain eye contact. Speak slowly and carefully, and articulate your sentences. Be honest. If you tell them you know a certain programming language, be prepared to back it up with experience and know-how. If you don't know a programming language they might ask you about, be honest. Tell them you are not fluent with that particular program, but you are a fast learner, and am willing to do what it takes to learn the ropes. Then stress your pluses. For instance, you could tell them that although you may not know the programming language they were looking for, you do know other languages such as (fill in the blank with your favorite fast food products and cookie brand names).

3.2.3.1 The College System

Chances are good that there's a local community or city college where classes cost between $10 to $50 per unit in your area. So go and sign up for any class that seems semi interesting, preferably having to do with computers and web development, but even underwater basket weaving 101 will do. Not only will this give you great experience in weaving baskets at 30 fathoms for minimal out-of-pocket expense, but will also give you an excellent opportunity to hit up instructors about their web sites. This is the absolute best chance for you to develop your skills as a web designer while having the option of adding to your resume, 'Volunteer Web Designer for BertnerVille College' where of course you can then offer examples of your work and what you accomplished and chances are in your favor that you'll get an 'A', even if you never touched the homework!

Instructors need web sites because it's a great chance for them to look ahead of the game, and most importantly because it's helpful. They can post a message board for students, offer critical class information that might have been left out of the syllabus, offer a copy of their syllabus, class schedule, office hours, email address, phone numbers, links to their favorite research tools or information. I'm sure that the college has given them a generic web page with minimal information, but that's where you will shine! Go around to different instructors and professors. Ask them about their current web site or whether they even have one yet. Tell them you are in a position to develop their site simply as a volunteer service to their department. Explain that you are a student at the college in training, and that you need to practice your web development skills. Since it's a win/win situation for both of you, there should not be any resistance. Sometimes they'll say something to the effect of, 'Thanks but I have someone working on it now'. To which you can say ask, "Who? Where do I find them? Can I assist them?". Or they might say, 'The college handles this already'. To which you can enquire, "What department handles this? Whom should I speak with?". Basically you want to get as much information as possible for possible leads or contacts. Be prepared to conduct some investigation in making progress towards volunteering. Some colleges even have a volunteer office where you can make enquiries about developing web sites. As a student, you will also have full access to their job center, where you can utilize their resources to finding new projects to help enhance your web designer skills.

3.2.3.2 The Public and Private Schools

The great thing about approaching local district schools and private schools is that they generally require funding for everything. This is advantages to you as a volunteer representative who wishes to teach web skills to youth, or help develop school based web sites. Depending on the kind of person you are though, you may find that there's a pro and a con to volunteering for schools. The pro is that you'll be working with children. The con is that you'll be working with children. It's usually best to volunteer alternative services (library assistant or teachers aid) to start so you can at least get in the front door. This will put you in a great position to learn what kind of help is needed on the web end. You can then make suggestions to the management as to how you could assist at a volunteer level with their difficulties and expand your increasing expertise in web development.

3.2.3.3 The Libraries and Public Buildings

Get familiar with your local city Chamber of Commerce. If you call for general information on volunteering, you might not get suitable answers concerning your services at a web level. Therefore it's usually best to find out what the cities web site address is, and possibly whether they have contact information for you such as a name or phone number of the administrator in charge of the web content. It's possible that the site is outsourced to a third-party, in which case you might need to look for other alternatives. However, there's also a chance that the city runs an in-house web team, which is your ticket to volunteering your web services.

Set up an appointment with whomever supervises the web team. Let them know that you are a student in training, and would like the opportunity to volunteer your services. The best part about spending free time with a real web team is that you will learn what process they use to push projects through the pipeline. This is important because there are several different content management styles, where many different tools and methods are applied. It's best that you get exposure to many different formats and situations, as it is all part of the learning and saturation process.

3.2.3.4 Networking through Friends and Family

Chances are good that you know someone who knows someone who needs a web site built at an economical rate. Tell them that since they are friends of friends, that you'll give them a special rate. Be casual but aggressive, and follow-up with those you make offers to. If you're still in the beginning stages, offer to setup mockup screens of different content styles of web sites for them free of charge. This way you can get practice, build your portfolio, and get good publicity. See, it works like this—For every person you help, they will refer you to 10 more people who will refer you to 10 more people, and so on. However, if you treat the person poorly by over charging, or simply not showing results, then you can bet that your contact is going to tell 20 people to stay away from you, who will then tell 20 more people to stay away from you, and so forth. Basically you can work hard at taking one step forward, or fudge it terribly and take two steps back, which means you would have to work twice as hard to get out of the negative. Although I didn't excel in mathematics, I can assure you that being in the negative with a client is a bad thing, especially if they are contacts that come from friends or relatives. Work especially hard at keeping these clients happy.

3.2.3.5 On the Job Experience

If you are currently working in another field, other than web development, chances are good that someone either has worked on a web site for your company, or currently is working on your company website. If you work for a larger corporation, there's a chance that your company runs an entire web team. This is a great opportunity to take a stroll in their general direction and make some new friends. Best thing about working for the same company is that you usually have something immediately in common (although they may get a little defensive and ask what you think you're doing just strolling around on their turf, at which point they might corner you, pull out switchblades, then ask you to please hand over your lunch money if it's not too much trouble). It's best to proceed with caution if you choose to simply walk into their domain and say 'Hi'. Leave your lunch money safely at your desk.

If you work for a smaller company, they may not even have a web site up and running yet, or may even have a web site but of very cheesy quality. Both of which are great situations for yourself. Introduce the idea of having a web site. Offer to manage the site content. Be prepared to show costs, and describe in detail how you would propose to manage the content. If they have a current web site of cheesy quality, simply mockup a couple of screen shots in Adobe Photoshop, showing the before and after views, then offer to show them to management. Tell them you have a cost effective way of redesigning the web site that will offer a better interface, and ultimately receive more hits from users. Then display your mockups.

3.2.3.6 Corporations

Should you decide to approach corporations, other than the ones you may currently work for, it's best to approach them as an intern in training. The best part about offering your services as an intern is that the corporation gets free labor out of you while you get on the job training. Plus you get to list their corporate name on your resume which is a great plus when building resume experience. Some internships pay, but they usually require that you've already had experience in web development and/or design, or they may require your current enrollment at a University with a couple years at school under your belt, portfolio in hand, and a solid major in Design or Computer Science. But it's always worth asking about. Don't simply decide that it's not worth your time until you've taken some time to find out what the real deal is. The other great thing about corporate internship is that they lead to possible employment opportunities within the company once you've spent some time with them. From their point of view, you already work with the staff, are highly trained, and have proven skills. From your point of view, you get to make great contacts, learn management skills, and possibly new technologies as you learn to grapple their content system. If you'd like a humorous look at corporate life, I'd recommend that you rent the movie Office Space from your local video store.

3.2.3.7 Non Profit Organizations

Although having a title such as 'Save the Platypus Association' on your resume may not be your cup of tea, it does have its pluses. Non Profit Organizations depend largely on donations, but also depend heavily on administration from volunteers and others. Having good representation is vital, which is where your skills as a web designer come in to play. A web site enables these organizations to advertise their goals while soliciting for donations via electronic commerce. Although you might not get paid for your assistance, your skills would more than likely be very welcome. Many Non profit Organizations depend on sponsorships from larger companies and usually maintain strong contact networking through many high profile sources such as lobbyist groups, think tanks, corporations, media and entertainment industry, etc...This is a great way for you to get experience with your skills, and network to other sources. You're always selling your skills whether on the job or not, and contact networking is virtually the key to opening other closed doors.

Your local library should have a book listing all local organizations including addresses and phone numbers. You could try your local telephone pages also. If you still cannot find a good index of organizations, you might consider contacting your local district United States House Representative, and ask their staff how you might obtain a list of Non Profit Organizations in your immediate area.

3.2.3.8 Government and Procurement Opportunities

Getting a job with the government can be an intimidating process. For instance, it's my understanding that in order to meet their strict employment requirements, you must fill out a form that can only be found in the attic of Beatrice Taylor's home, which burned down years ago. She is a former postal employee in Nantucket who stole the form from the Top Secret Department of the Pentagon. Then you must sign the form using ONLY a number .01 pencil lead, in the area of the form that states 'Office Use Only'. This form must then be hand delivered by the prospective employee to Ruth at the Library in Cali, Wyoming along with the required $800.00 processing fee by 2pm yesterday.

However, I have an alternate method to getting in good with the government. The process is called procurement, and it's the same as consulting. Basically the government only has so much money to go around for different projects, which are then outsourced to the lowest bidder. The terrific part is that anyone can bid on these projects if they are an established D.B.A (Doing Business As). You can become a D.B.A by visiting your local City Chamber of Commerce where you will be required to pay a registration amount and fill out some light paperwork (as opposed to heavy paperwork).

Once you're a D.B.A, you can apply for a business account at the bank of your choice, get company checks, and write off business related expenses for tax purposes. Plus you don't even have to spend time debating over a company name, as it could simply be your name DBA, like this: John Doe DBA.

In order to compete for different projects, you need to visit *http://www.eps.gov* and fill out their one time online registration form. You will then have the ability to conduct RFQ's (Request for Quotes) of any open business opportunities over and under $25,000 within many of the Government Agencies. Many Agencies are conveniently centralizing their opportunities in the EPS database which is short for General Services Administration Electronic Posting System.

You might find that some projects are out of your league as some government procurement opportunities require that the bidder have an established business with employees. So long as you carefully read the description of what's required to fulfill the contract, you'll find many that are right up your alley.

3.2.3.9 Online Job Auction Websites

Freelancing for certain project work in the Internet industry is a terrific way to gain a strong foothold in the ever evolving community. The problem for some companies in the Internet industry is a lack of funding or work opportunities for full-time employees. For many companies that only want someone to tackle a certain project over a very short period of time, it seems logical to hire a freelancer as a consultant (especially over hiring a consultant from an established firm where the billing rate can be astronomically high, ranging anywhere from $150 to $350 per hour).

The problem for the web designer is finding someplace that has constant information on freelance projects as they become available. That's where *http://www.elance.com*, *http://www.guru.com*, *http://www.freeagent.com* and eFrenzy come into play. These websites are consortiums where companies list projects, and web designers from all over the world bid on projects. They're not just for web designers though. Projects can vary from graphic design to Furby Mechanics and general advice/counsel on all sorts of topics, but for the sake of argument, we'll just focus on the web designer aspect of these groovy websites.

E-lancing (freelancing with an electronic medium) as it's coined is a great way to gain vital experience if you live in an area of the world where it's difficult enough just to find a local grocery store, let alone a local Dot Com company or other that's in desperate need of web services. E-lancing gives you the chance to shine like a star by working at home on projects that might be initiated across the globe.

The downside though is that it's not a dependable source of constant income. I highly recommend this method for resume experience, however don't expect to earn a living by staying home and working on projects that might be happening in Madagascar. First off, you'll usually be competing for the temporary contract with other extremely talented web designers from all over the world. Secondly, the projects won't necessarily provide a sound financial solution to paying the bills and putting bread on the table. The fact is that companies are going to where they can get cheap talent quick. They are usually most worried about their bottom line, and will in most cases hire the cheapest talent that can get the job done.

3.3 Expand Your Vocabulary

One of the things you'll learn about the web world is that language is essential. If you can't describe a problem or solution using the proper syntax to others in the industry, you're going to be in a heap of trouble. First off, web designers usually interact with programmers and back-end developers. Programmers and back-end developers need to know in precise terminology what needs to be done to accommodate you.

Here's an example of a flawed conversation that's not going work:

Web Guy: I need you to make a file for the web site.

Programmer: Hmmm. What kind of file?

Web Guy: Um…One that gives me a name I can use to get stuff from the storage thingy.

Programmer: I see. What storage thingy are you referring to?

Web Guy: You know, the one that stores all the information and stuff.

Programmer: No, I don't know. We have different storage mediums. Are you referring to the SQL (pronounced See—Quill) database?

Web Guy: Of course I am! That's what I meant…I need a name from SeaGull.

Programmer: (Prays that it's lunchtime as he looks at his watch) Do you need to return a string or a numeric value, and from which table?

Web Guy: Look, all I know is that I need a name from SeaGull.

Programmer: (opens the nearest window) I can't take it anymore!!!

Web Guy: No, please don't jump! I still need work from you!

Programmer: Who said anything about **ME** jumping? (Grabs the Web Guy and pushes him towards the open window)

Web   Guy: But   what   about   the   file   I   need   from   Sea…AHHHHHhhhhhhhhhhhhhhhhhhhhhhhh! (Splat!)

Not very effective, except for the Programmer, who got to take an early lunch. Let's now take a look at a much more effective conversation:

Web Guy: I need a variable called $MyVar1 that returns the $DisplayResults string from the Results Table in SQL.

Programmer: When do you need it by?

Web Guy: The project needs to be completed by Friday, but I can handle the other routines and come back to this one when you're done. Can you have this done by noon tomorrow?

Programmer: OK. Send me an email outlining the specifications, and I'll get on it.

Web Guy: Gee, thanks!

The first example was extreme. It hopefully got you thinking about the importance of knowing how to effectively apply the language, or at the very least thinking about Newton's Law of Gravity. The only true way to apply the lingo properly is to have a base understanding and appreciation for the tools that the programmers and back-end developers use. This will help you talk effectively to others that you work with, and will also give you a better understanding of how programming tools can help you accomplish your goals.

3.3.1 Taking Classes

If you have a local community college nearby, I strongly suggest that you find out which computer courses they offer. The terrific thing about a community college is the cost. You can get into a class for usually $10 to $25 per unit. Each class is usually three to five units. You could take a weekend class only, or put together a class schedule that works around your life. But, you will definitely learn the terminology and gain valuable skills that could come in handy. For instance, if you take a SQL class, you will learn all about database administration, which would look terrific on your resume! Many a web designer has gotten into the Internet industry simply because they understand and can work with a database language. Taking classes will broaden your skills, and make you a much more robust web designer. I would suggest that you take some courses on server maintenance, so you can learn how to work with a web server, a class in CGI and JAVA, Photoshop and Interface Design.

3.3.2 Getting Certified

One of the best ways to sell an employer on your ability to create and maintain exceptional web content is to have certifications in one or more web tools. There are many programs available, depending on the language or skill you wish to become certified in including programs such as Microsoft Certified Web Engineer training, or Java training through Sun, or Oracle database training through Oracle. Just keep in mind that certification is expensive and usually requires that you throw money to the wind for several months until eventually you receive a nice piece of paper at the end of your training, that makes it all worth while! There are usually two approaches to completing certification.

The first way entails you finding suitable classes that are presented by a certification center nearest you. Basically, you would need to contact the main vender for training information on their product line to find information on where and when they will be holding their next series of classes. Be prepared to pay top dollar for these certification programs though, as they can last anywhere from a single day course to several months, including expenses for books, training, and testing.

The second way is to simply visit your local bookstore and purchase the training and exercise books for the particular certification program you are most interested in. You would still need to contact the vender to find information on their certification programs, but in this case you would be home schooling. Then when you feel you are ready to tackle the tests, you would find the nearest certification testing facility. This can get costly as well, considering you will be paying for books, training manuals, and testing.

Certification is not meant to take the place of a college degree, and should not be viewed as such. It is a way though to add expertise in one or more given web tools on your resume. Plus it will make you that much more sellable to clients, and will also give you the experience that is necessary in making prudent and professional web content decisions.

3.3.3 Reading Books and eBooks

If you haven't guessed it yet, you are currently reading an ebook (electronic book). Books and web development go hand in hand, and it's important that you at least visit your local bookstore or online ebook retailer, to look at the vast number of resources available to you in this new field of work. You will find resource guides on everything from programming languages to utilizing color palettes more efficiently. As a web designer, be prepared to start a library on issues ranging from web usability, layout and design, to reference manuals on HTML, JavaScript and the like. It's true that many of these resources are available for free on the internet, and if you can find suitable materials to fulfill your needs, then more power to you. I would still maintain a personal reference library though considering how difficult it can be to find certain information on development.

3.3.4 Keeping Up with Technology

It's important that you keep up with current events in web technology. I strongly suggest that you resist the urge to use every new technology in your development of web sites (mostly because it takes a while for the majority of web users to download the plug-in for the new technology to work with their browsers). But I definitely suggest that you spend quality time getting up to speed with what tools are being developed for your benefit. It will give you a good sense of direction for where the web might be going in the coming months or years, will broaden your insight as to what is available in the way of site content tools, and will make you that much more the wiser.

Pay careful attention to trends in Internet and Web related technology. One way is to read the Technology section of NewsWeek Magazine. Another way is to visit *http://www.cnet.com*, which is fairly accurate in terms of technology and direction. You will find many resources that can assist you in this endeavor, so it's best that you search for materials that are suiting to your needs, then maintain a regiment approach at studying emerging technologies and trends in the market.

3.3.5 Practice Makes Permanent

Above all else though, spend a large majority of your time simply doing. It's important that you practice your skills whenever possible. For one thing, it will keep the information that you learn fresh in your head. For another thing, it gives you content to add to your expanding portfolio of work. Even if you conduct basic exercises every once in a while to test your skills, it will help you become a more efficient and thorough designer. Spend time with Photoshop learning the keystroke commands, as you will find it drastically speeds up your ability to create mockups and graphics. Spend time writing HTML and JavaScript content to keep the commands fresh in your memory. Practice formatting tables and aligning a web page so that you can refine your Interface development skills. So long as you keep active in fine-tuning your web skills, you will find yourself more confident and marketable.

4. WELCOME TO THE BIG TIME!

If you've gotten this far in your reading then chances are good that you are ready for the crash course in finding work within the Internet industry as a (drum role please...) WEB DESIGNER! Take a bow, you deserve it.

4.1 What Jobs Are Out There?

You will find that Internet jobs abound all over the nation. Chances are good that in your neck of the woods alone, there are Internet companies sprouting out of the ground, and growing abundantly. If you are interested in checking local listings, I suggest that you visit either *http://www.techies.com* or *http://www.monster.com* where if you conduct a keyword search for 'web developer', 'web designer', 'web producer', 'UI designer', or 'UI developer' you will find something about roughly as close to home as your local McDonalds.

If not, don't fret little pilgrim! There are plenty of exotic locations to choose from, such as Salt Lake City Utah, Boston Massachusetts, New York City, Virginia, Portland Oregon, Texas, and of course California. Which brings me to...

4.1.1 Where is Silicon Valley?

Chances are good that regardless of whether you're a techie or not, you've heard something somewhere down the line about Silicon Valley. It's where herds of programmers flock to annually and settle for the season. In fact, Silicon Valley is actually a magical land where extremely geeky technical wizards mysteriously evolve into Porsche driving, millionaires.

Located just a tad West of San Francisco, it all begins on Sand Hill Road. Mostly because that's the street where all the big wig venture-capital firms are located. And in the Internet industry, it all starts with a terrific idea and lots of cash (provided by the generous dwellers on Sand Hill Road). Silicon Valley is also home to many veteran Hi-Tech companies such as Excite, Netscape, Sun Microsystems, Apple, idealab! and others. The climate is cool, and the streets are paved in gold (not really, but wouldn't that make for an exciting little town?!).

4.1.2 Where are the MIT Gurus and Top Executives Going?

In actuality, many of them aren't going very far from home. The Internet industry is flourishing in almost every city across the nation. The reason for this is the flexibility in setting up shop and building an online product. One company rented a mansion and conducted 'business as usual' within it's nineteenth century rooms complete with a sales, marketing, programming, and business development divisions (not surprisingly, the company was launching an online product!).

The latest trend in the Internet & Dot Com community though is the warehouse effect, where they build technology companies complete with gazillion dollar architecture, lighting and air conditioning, in old run down warehouses. Doesn't look like much when you see it from the outside, but usually the deco is enough to blow your mind away when you walk into the entry way (usually complete with fountains, bridges, stand up arcades, and the like...).

Many of the experienced Dot Com employees are moving on to companies that are one step ahead of the trends in the Industry. At this particular time, there are three major shifts in the Internet Industry. One is B2B, which stands for Business to Business where a Dot Com company provides services only for other businesses, and not the basic constituent class of consumers. The second major shift is free internet access. Companies like NetZero, Juno, and others offer free access to the Internet in exchange for the ability to display advertisements while connected. The third major shift is wireless. Many companies are taking their products to cellular phones and Palm Pilots which have access to the Internet. The Internet industry is always evolving, so it's hard to pinpoint where the market is definitely going to go, but now's a great time to move into several different strategic situations that will prove beneficial down the road, as these trends continue to evolve.

4.1.3 What's an Incubation Company?

Idealab! (*http://www.idealab.com*) And CMGI (*http://www.cmgi.com*) are only a couple examples of incubators that have tried to take the Internet industry to the next level. In some cases, such as Cars Direct (*http://www.carsdirect.com*) and NetZero (*http://www.netzero.net*) they've very much succeeded, but in other cases, such as the long gone iExchange.com (*http://www.iexchange.com*) and IceBox (http://www.ice-box.com) were failures, having burned through their funding and closed their doors for good. The idea is that incubation companies would provide capital funding for Dot Com startups and provide a facilitated network, housing, phones, desks, equipment, and sodas to those Dot Com companies which are in the crucial first few months of life (until the Dot Com startup is grown up enough to spread its wings and 'leave the nest'). Incubators provide excellent resources such as 401k's and medical coverage for most employees working within their umbrella. In exchange for all these wonderful resources, an incubator will usually walk away with a fair amount of equity in the Dot Com startup, as well as a large voice as to how the product is rolled out. When the Dot Com startup has aggressively launched its product, and filed the Security Exchange Commission (SEC) paperwork to take the company public (that is to say, publicly traded on the stock market), the incubator will then be able to cash in its equity and make a substantial profit.

108 •   B e c o m i n g a W e b D e s i g n e r...

I strongly suggest checking with the incubation companies as they are always in need of strong web talent. Although idealab! and CMGI aren't the only two incubation companies in the world, they are two of the largest, most prestigious and well financed operations in the industry. I would advise that you weigh your options heavily though when choosing one incubation startup from the next. Many of the startups are founded on conceptually brilliant ideas, but some simply have a goal of filling a gap on the Internet that's currently vacant. Just keep in mind that some Dot Com companies can be potential 'Hit and Miss' operations that are only trying to cash out on a quick idea. The best way to avoid hazardous situations like this is to critically study the market of your future employer. Don't accept any job offers from within the incubation community without understanding the risks first. Ask direct questions about the startup company, such as who's the competition, what kind of growth potential exists in that particular market, and then decide for yourself whether or not you think their idea has the potential to make big dollars.

4.1.4 Average Pay Rates

What I'd like say is that all web designers are millionaires, and don't rely on salaries or wages because they are filthy rich. However, that would be stretching the truth just a wee bit. The actuality of it all, from a realistic perspective is that most web designers that work in the Internet environment make great monetary sacrifices in the hopes that their company has what it takes to go public so they can cash out their stock options. Generally, $30,000 to $50,000 is acceptable with anywhere from 5,000 to 30,000 shares (These figures are only based on a web designer who has standard working knowledge and basic web experience). Although you will have a tighter salary, your stock will be worth considerably more if your company files for an Initial Public Offering, because your stock price is based on the company value at the time the shares are issued to you. Therefore, if you are working for a startup Dot Com company worth

$30,000,000, your stock purchase price will probably be somewhere around $.10 cents per share! Think about it…Even if your company tanks after going IPO, and only jumps to $10.00 per share, you could still walk away with $300,000.00 if you initially purchased 30,000 shares. That's quite a profit.

It can also be considered quite a loss. You've got to remember that you are bound to pay taxes on all stock that you sell. If you purchase your shares though, and hold on to them for 2 years before selling, then the IRS considers that to be a long term investment, in which you would qualify for capital gains which could save you up to 35% in penalties should you decide to sell earlier than the 2 year mark (from the date of purchase).

If you work for an established corporation (usually non Dot Com related, as most Dot Com companies have yet to establish themselves), you can secure a much better salary, such as $50,000 to $90,000 (depending on your experience, abilities, interviewing skills, and who you know). You will more than likely receive stock options as well. The standard amount of equity issued is 10% of your annual salary (this can vary depending on the company and the circumstances.) Although you will have more secure employment, as the corporation usually has deeper pockets, your stock will probably cost more money to purchase, depending on what the stock price was at on your first day of hire.

4.1.5 Researching Upcoming Trends in the Marketplace

One of the things that you need to consider is consumer and investor interest. As it is, several Internet companies are folding and going bankrupt simply because they can't make a profit. There was a time when investors didn't even bother to look at the expense reports of Internet companies. They simply poured money into Internet companies that had the most potential in e-markets that were vacant. However this trend has since come to a grinding halt, as investors have become increasingly more particular about Internet technology and the Internet industry in general. Even companies on the Internet that have proven their ability to make a profit are finding themselves in a tough spot as people are more concerned with the market at large, and therefore aren't willing to risk capital investments in companies who aren't showing a solid ROI (Return On Investment).

There is a happy ending to this story though. As those Internet companies that can't make it in the big league continue to be weeded out, and forced to sell out or go bankrupt, there will be left standing a few that have shown their ability to thrive on consumer demand. This will lead to increased sales, stronger profits, established e-corporations, solid growth in the marketplace, and will thus make many new millionaires.

One of the ways you can stay in tune with current Internet events is to read NewsWeek Magazine. The great thing about NewsWeek is that they have a tendency to cover current trends in the Internet Industry. Also, take time to frequent the C-net website (*http://www.cnet.com*). They usually have terrific articles on emerging technologies, current position of the Internet marketplace, and what's down the road.

Spend time paying attention to current events. Global events affect the world at large, much like dropping a rock into a calm, shallow pool of water. Ripples will thrust away from the epicenter and bring chaotic activity to the once calmer waters. If you keep up with global and technological events, I can guarantee that you'll be able to answer with conviction, one of the most common interview questions, which is this. "Where do you see the Internet in 5 years?"

4.1.6 What Should I Be Looking For in a Company?

Basically, you should want to be associated with a company that you feel would be a strong reference on your resume. Remember that the company you work with reflects strongly on you later down the line. If you decide to work for a pornographic Internet company for instance, simply because of the high hopes of their stock going public, this might not necessarily help you later down the road when you present your resume and portfolio to your interviewer.

Although it can be extremely difficult, it's usually best to start out in the industry with a company that's going to give you the exposure you need to the project based work environment. If the company is run out of a house or garage, you should ask yourself whether you are looking to gain valuable experience that will improve your skills as a web designer. For instance, will you have the opportunity to work with other divisions such as marketing, sales, quality engineering (or quality assurance), and Development.

If the company is a brand new startup, you should consider stability. Chances are good that you could be out of work pretty quick if the company doesn't have a product that sounds like it's going to be a winner. Ask yourself about the product they are offering. Is there an audience for their services? How will they make profits? How much money will it take them to realistically meet their goals, and do they have a strong team that can pull it off. Don't be afraid to ask the company direct questions. After all, it's your life. Considering that you will spend a majority of your time under their roof, working for them, it's important that you feel 100% confident about them before you dedicate your time and energy to them.

If they are a corporation, is there room for advancement? What is the management team like, and what is their management style? What kind of benefits are being offered. I can tell you upfront that in the Internet Industry, it's just about standard for the company to offer you catered breakfast, lunch and/or dinner, free sodas and vending machines, standard benefits, and great perks such as a gym, or company sponsored athletic events, or Playroom including a Sony Playstation, lots of video games, air hockey, and/or a pool table.

How close to home is this job, and how much driving will you have to do? What kind of hours are they expecting from you. Most Internet companies don't have you clock in or clock out of work. You are usually salary based, and are given a fairly flexible work schedule provided that you complete your duties professionally and on time.

Also, a good thing to look at is their competition. Do they have any competitors? If they do, what is their competition offering in the way of employment. Then compare the differences. Also look seriously at how your company is going to compete on the open market. This will give you some indication as to how they conduct business, and what they are all about. Just remember that knowledge is power. Information builds confidence, and confidence wins in the interview stage.

4.1.7 Finding Brand Spanking New Companies

Finding Internet companies can be a frustrating experience, if you don't know where to look. You could start with the Newspaper Classified section, but this can prove to be an unvaluable frustration, as you have to filter through so many none Internet related positions (provided you are lucky enough to find any at all!).

Fortunately, there are resources on the Internet that can assist you in finding vacant positions in the Industry. Two websites I strongly recommend are *http://www.monster.com* and *http://www.techies.com*. Each of which provide detailed listings that relate to the Internet industry. You can conduct a keyword search for any of the following items to receive relevant information that will help you zero in on your target, such as "UI Designer", "UI Developer","Web Designer","Web Developer", "Web Producer", etc...

Another way to find positions of employment in the Internet industry is to simply visit the websites that interest you most, then find a link that relates to Employment (usually you need to click through 'About Us' before you find a jobs link).

4.1.7.1 Word of Mouth

If you can honestly say that you don't know a single person in the industry, then this is a great time to go out to meet people with similar interests. I'm not suggesting that you go date someone that's already on the inside (although that would help!☺). I am however suggesting that you research community clubs, and find out when and where computer or Internet clubs meet. A lot of times it's not what you know, but who you know that counts. Even if your new friends don't prove useful, you will gain valuable insight as to how the Industry language is spoken, and it will definitely put you in the center of current high technology debates ranging from computer hardware, to video games and online commerce.

4.1.7.2 The Incubators

Remember the Dot Com incubation companies such as CMGI (*http://www.cmgi.com*) and idealab! (*http://www.idealab.com*)? These are great websites to visit when enquiring about prospective employment. They usually display openings with several Dot Com companies all over the world. Simply find the position that most appeals to you, then research the Dot Com company itself to make sure it's everything you're looking for. Just keep in mind that if you're new to the industry, beggars can't be choosers. You might need to suck in your gut, and simply dive into what ever you can get. Even if that means working in a dirty basement, so that you can develop exciting new online commerce services that provide important products such as Llama treats. Just get into a position, gain the needed experience, ramp up your portfolio, then get out and go elsewhere. The best thing about the industry is that you aren't expected to stay with a Dot Com company very long, which is why many of them usually cater extra employee benefits and perks just to keep you excited and interested in your work.

4.1.7.3 Eyes Wide Open

Whatever method you decide to use in finding work within the Internet industry (and I suggest that you employ as many tactics as possible in your quest for the ultimate web designer position), I urge you to take your blinders off. In other words, don't get so focused on one course of action that you completely ignore other avenues that might lead down the same path. For instance, you could easily find yourself in a café with a cup of juice and a newspaper classified section, struggling to find a solid lead, while the whole time, the café you are seated in is struggling to get its menu online. Just because it seems that every mother, brother, daughter and dog has an Internet website, you shouldn't dismiss the idea that most small to mid-sized companies have yet to transition to the Internet. Many of them are aching to get online, but haven't a clue where to start, or how to find someone within their budget that can help. Potential opportunity brushed aside simply because you were focused on that café cup and classified section.

Finally, remember also that sitting around isn't going to cut it. It's not like companies are thinking to themselves, 'gee, I wonder if Billy Bob is in his trailer today. We really need to get a website up and golly whiz, I'm just in the mood to give him a check for a million dollars if he'll accept my job offer. I'll give him a call right now. No! Better yet, I'll send a limo to pick him up.'…If it were that simple, I wouldn't have to spend my precious video game playing hours writing this book! You need to be pro-active. It takes determination, will power, and hard work. So get your hands dirty, and start digging in the mud. Somewhere under all that soil, is a treasure with your name on it!

4.2 Getting in the Front Door

Getting in the front door should be pretty simple right? After all, you only need to brush your hair, and walk through the front door with a smile. They should naturally be begging you to come back and work for them! Unfortunately though, it's not quite that simple. It takes a lot of preparation work on your part to ensure that you are equal to the challenge of presentation.

4.2.1 The Good 'Ol Resume

Your resume is a lot like your personal trophy case, displaying all your finest accomplishments in life, which pertain to the job in which you are applying. I'm not going to give you a course in building a resume or cover letter, however I strongly suggest that you visit *http://www.monster.com* where you will find intuitive information and examples concerning proper resume building. My best advice on catering to your resume, is to be bold. If for instance, you helped a friend build a basic website, and it looks good, then don't be bashful and leave it out thinking it's not important for the interviewer to see…Be Bold! Put it on the resume with finesse! For example, "Web Site Designer: Helped develop constituent web site. Created mockups in Photoshop 5.5, scripted site using HTML formatted complex tables and JavaScript."

Some people have a tendency to turn a one page resume into a book complete with table of contents and index. While it's important that you stress your most applicable work, it's also important that you filter what's on your resume so that you are putting only your best achievements down on paper, that relate to the job in which you are applying.

4.2.2 Submitting Your Portfolio

In Web design, it's extremely important that you keep an up-to-date portfolio of all your work, including notes, sketches, and printed HTML for previous content and graphics. Where your resume gets you in the front door, the portfolio secures your job! A director will be most interested in seeing your design aesthetics, such as the layout, color palette, alignment, formatting, text sizes, proportion, font types, graphic sizes and resolution, width of the page (fixed or dynamic folding width), among many other aspects. This gives you a great chance to discuss with your interviewer why you chose to develop a page in the manner that you did, what you liked best and worst about your work, and what you might have done differently had you been given the opportunity.

Keep a copy of your HTML handy as well, since this gives the interviewer a chance to see how easy your scripting is to read. You've got to think of scripting in the same terms as poetry, in that everyone has a different and unique writing style. There are certain rules that apply to scripting HTML, such as specific attributes that must be used with consistency: your spaces, style, remark statements and flow will determine whether it's easily readable by another person who might have to work with your style of scripting on the job when you're hired.

Many people feel as though they don't have a 'proper' portfolio unless it's contained within an expensive leather portfolio case, or the like. I've always used a basic manila folder, and have found that it works wonders, while saving lots of money that could go elsewhere. If you really want to look cool, go to a local art supply store and get yourself a professional portfolio case. All I'm saying though is that it's not necessary to get the perfect job.

4.2.3 Email Vs. Contact Calling

So far, I've worked for two different companies where all pre-interview communication was handled strictly by email only. I had sent my resume to the company, then they had emailed me a week later asking whether I was still interested. I replied via email stating that I was interested in meeting, and they had replied back with an interview schedule and directions. It's extremely convenient to relay information via email, and shows some of your web savvy skills before you've even interviewed for the position!

If someone gives you an email address, it's probably to your benefit that you maintain an electronic address book complete with a reference of all email addresses that are work related. In many cases, you may not get a job from a specific company, but if you check back with the company contact via email later down the line, it could prove to be a wise time investment on your part, and they could prove a useful reference for future jobs. Just because a company says 'No.', that really should be translated to mean

'Not yet.' (unless of course there are several police officers with guns drawn on the scene, in which case 'No' probably really means 'NO!').

4.2.4 Being Represented

One of the most stress free ways of establishing interviews, is to have representation. This means that you have a person that works to assist you in finding solid employment contacts. One type of representation is through headhunters. They usually get hired by large firms to steal good employment from other large firms. Another type of representation is through IT Placement firms such as Romac International (*http://www.romac.com*), where they screen their applicants to ensure they are finding good matches for the applicants field of expertise. The upside is that they have a lot more contacts with employers on the inside than you might, and have strong credibility with many companies. The downside is that you can't expect undivided attention from a placement consultant. They usually represent several applicants looking to find employment just like you. Plus you will need to keep on good terms through constant communication with them so that you are always on the top of their A list.

4.2.5 Open Houses and Job Fairs

Since the field of Web Development is still in its infancy and unsaturated, many Internet companies host Job Fairs and Open Houses to lure the talent their way. It's best that you dress to impress when you go though, and that you bring your resume and portfolio along for the ride. Always be prepared! Trade shows are good contact sources, such as Comdex. Make sure to collect as many business cards as possible, as most of them will offer email addresses that make as good inside contact sources for employment opportunities.

How popular and in demand are job fairs? NetZero Corporation, a banner driven free Internet Service Provider, recently had an Open House that attracted over 1,500 net savvy people like yourself. They were hiring for positions in many different fields, however it's not unusual for an Internet company to have lines wrapped around the building just to get into the Open House or Job Fair. Don't get discouraged though, just remember that you are the best! Now all you have to do is convince the Internet companies, and you're all set!

4.3 The Interview

Just remember that in much as they are interviewing you, that you in fact should be just as inclined to interview them in return. Ask good 'find out' questions that will ultimately lead to important information that might help you decide whether to accept the job later down the line. It will also display enthusiasm and interest that will rub off in your favor! Here are some questions that might be useful to ask...

1. How many employees currently work for your company?
2. What kind of benefits and perks are available to the employees?
3. Do you have an air hockey table?
4. What about free lunch and/or dinner?
5. Do you have health insurance, and will I be charged to enroll my family?
6. Will I have the option of requisitioning for computer equipment, such as a 21" monitor, speakers, video card, zip drive, the latest version of Photoshop, or laser optic mouse (beats the roller ball, trust me!).
7. What holidays do you honor?
8. Will I receive stock option benefits?
9. Are children allowed in the workplace?
10. Do you have a Nintendo? ☺

11. Are the people here very friendly?

12. Are fish tanks allowed?

13. Where do you see this company in 5 years?

14. What deals are currently in the works, that will ensure your companies success?

15. Do you offer bonuses for job referrals? (This one will perk their ears right up! They love hiring people who are excited enough about the company and outgoing enough to encourage friends, relatives and others to join as well!!!)

Keep in mind that you can take these questions any way you want to. The point that I'm making is that it's important you ask direct questions that put the interviewer on the spot so that you have as much information before making a decision one way or another.

What about on there end? What can you expect, question wise from the gurus of hiring?

16. What did you like about your last job?

17. Why did you quit your last job?

18. What's the hardest project you've encountered?

19. What skills can you bring to our successful team?

20. What programming languages have you worked with?

21. Where do you see the Industry in 5 years?

22. How much exposure do you have with web-based projects from conception to completion?

23. What do you know about our company?

24. How long have you been scripting HTML?

25. Do you know Photoshop?

26. What would you say, in your opinion, is your strongest trait?

27. What would you say, in your opinion, is your weakest trait?

28. What steps have you taken to strengthen your weakest trait?

29. What are your hobbies?

One bit of advice is this: When they ask you whether you've worked with a particular scripting language, don't lie. They can see through lies faster than you might think. Instead, be truthful, and confidently honest. If you really don't know a particular language, tell them right off the bat, "No. I don't know that particular language, however I'm a quick learner, and I do know the following languages, which are very close to what you are referring to...Blah, blah, blah..."

4.3.1 First Impressions

You only get one chance at making a first impression, so make it a good one! Don't walk in to an interview dressed like you missed the bus, and frantically chased it for two miles, through a rain storm, in the mud...See where this is going? Go in your best clothes, dress neat, make sure your clothes are ironed, and wear matching socks (Here's where listening to what your mother always told you comes in handy!). Brush your teeth, and shave. When the interviewer meets you, they will immediately categorize you into a mental stack of 'yes' or 'no' piles. They will politely listen to their 'no' pile, but the minute a 'no' person walks out the door, that person is mentally thrown out with the trash.

4.3.2 Enthusiasm and Energy

Walk in with confidence, and hold your head up high. Always make eye contact. Speak slowly and articulately. Be polite, and offer a firm shake upon greeting and dismissal. But most importantly, SMILE!!!! ☺☺☺☺ See how these cute little happy faces are smiling? Doesn't it make you feel all tickled pink inside to see these smiling happy faces?! SMILE!!!! A smile will take you further, and bring you more success than any frown could ever muster. Even doctors say it's good for you, so don't go into an interview with a frown or scared look. Even if you spill juice on your nice shirt, get your tie stuck in the paper shredder, and loose a shoe to a rabid dog before your interview, just make sure that above all else, you go in there with a smile!

Do whatever it takes to ensure that your name is mentally placed in the interviewers 'yes' pile, or at the very least placed in their 'mental' list.

4.3.3 Know Your Vocabulary

At least a day before your interview is scheduled, take some time to review your materials, get your portfolio in order, and study computer terminology, and principles, so that your mind is already in tune. Take a long break after that, to let the information absorb, then get a good nights rest prior to the big day. Right before your interview, quickly go over the terminology to refresh your mind, and think about possible answers to directed interview type questions. Feel free to even talk out loud to yourself, by practicing the questions and answers. Say the terms so that they feel comfortable to you, and slide off your tongue with ease. Remember that Practice makes Permanent!

4.3.4 Who is Your Interviewer?

You've got to keep in mind that although they may sound totally interested in what you have to say in regards to their direct interview questions, the basic truth of the matter is that they are busy summing you up, while you are busy talking. This doesn't mean that they aren't listening to what you are saying...

For instance:

Interviewer: How would you describe your last job?

Grunt: Well, I can already tell that you aren't paying any attention to me at all...

Interviewer: mm-hmm. Good. Now then, What is your best trait?

Grunt: My, you look like a camel.

Interviewer: Can you go into more detail?

Grunt: Well, you are obviously not listening, so I'm just going to sing the national anthem, and call you sarcastic names afterwards, you big poopie head.

Interviewer: Wonderful. Did you learn from these experiences?

And so on, and so on....

Actually, we must give them much more credit than this, as they are really paying full attention to your every word, while at the same time, scoring your performance on a ticker sheet that will then be relayed back to management for the hiring decision. You are given numerical values, with some bit of thoughtful text to its side to score how well you do based on the following categories:

1. Enthusiasm
2. Level of Responsibility Held
3. Charisma
4. Decision making ability
5. Leadership ability

6. Eye contact

7. Articulate in speech and manner

8. Motivated

9. Detail oriented

10. Willingness to perform

11. Confidence Level

12. Sociable personality

I'm sure there are many other terms that can be added to this list. In fact, take a brief moment to reflect on these terms, and see if there aren't a few you can add to the list.

4.3.5 Selling Yourself as the Product

Remember that you are literally a salesman, representing and selling your skills to an employer. Imagine that you had to sell toothpicks to earn a living. First off, you'd have to be pretty persistent to sell toothpicks to some stranger on the street. You'd have to have determination, the ability to stay focused, and most importantly have a firm belief that others simply couldn't go on living another moment without your deluxe, gold leaf molded, mint flavored XLT extended length toothpicks. (Buy one now and get NONE free!). In a lot of ways, you've got to have the same determination and focus in place when you interview. Have confidence that you are the best, and that their company simply cannot ever be successful without your presence. Be bold, but not overbearing.

4.3.6 Negotiating On Your Own Terms

When you are applying for a job, one of the most common questions is what you are looking for salary wise. HAVE THIS ANSWER WELL PLANNED OUT IN ADVANCE! I can't force this issue enough, as I've seen it time and time again, when a terrific job candidate is asked the golden question. And they undersell themselves so that they can please the interviewer. This is simply the wrong approach. You should have the most confidence when you boldly state that you are looking for something in the ball park of...Now this is when it gets tricky. How do you judge the value of your skills? Unfortunately, In all my research, study, and meditation I have not found the perfect answer to this question. I have experience in this field of study though, as I've blundered my going rate, taken a job for a very low salary simply to get employed, only to discover later that they were prepared to pay between $20k to $30k more for the position, had I simply been bold and asked. Which proves to me that you get what you ask for. I finally got smart on this issue, and decided to shoot for a highly ludicrous (in my opinion) salary rate. They called me back with a job offer, and to top it off, they matched my salary request.

4.4 Accepting The Job

Well, now you've gone and done it. After all that hard work, you're finally at the finish line, which is to say that you have the golden key to the Internet restroom! Not to mention the cool credit card sized access card to the main entrance. So now that you've endured, and gotten to this wonderful stage in your web designer career, what can you expect from the inside of the Wonderful World of Web?!

4.4.1 Great Expectations

The first major thing you're going to notice is all the cool computer equipment. Usually the office is solely comprised of computer terminals, and desks complete with pictures of the family pet, lots of programming books, toys, etc...If you're lucky, you'll get your very own office, or cubicle. However, seeing as Internet companies tend to spend a majority of their funding on marketing, chances are better that you will probably have a simple make-shift desk made of a door minus the knob and hinges, laid over two cheap cabinets. Voilla, a desk!

Expect to move your belongings often, as your company will grow and expand to accommodate an exponential growth rate of new hires to accommodate the accelerated production growth of your key products.

You should also expect to spend between sixty to eighty hours in the office every week, and possibly more, as you will be one of the essential members of a team that is aggressively pushing a product to the marketplace.

Chances are good that you will probably end up working in a warehouse environment, which seems to be the latest fad in standardized environmental art deco within the Internet community.

Look forward also to wearing jeans, t-shirts, shorts and thongs to work as well. Just one of the many great perks when working in the Industry!

4.4.2 Order of Operations

An Internet company needs certain crucial elements to succeed. There's Marketing and Business Development, which pushes advertising to the constituent population of potential customers, establishes deals with third party vendors, sets up distribution deals, usually houses the design and creative staff for images, logos, colors, web (where you might work), studies market trends, sets forecasts for future earnings, secures the necessary capital for keeping the company running, creates promotions and contests to draw users, and the like.

There's Legal, which handles all the SEC paperwork for taking the company public (IPO), protects the companies interests, creates User Agreements, and maintains necessary legal paperwork.

Finance handles all the bills, e-commerce issues, bank negotiations, and employee pay.

Quality Assurance (QA for short) handles all the web site testing.

Customer Service handles customer complaints and escalations.

Sales are proactive and close the business deals to sell the products.

Some companies maintain a Creative segment that work to develop the user interface into a user friendly experience. This section is usually in place only when there's no Design team within the Marketing group.

Human Resources makes sure that there's always a pool of candidates to draw from in expanding the companies employment numbers. They also handle benefits, such as tax forms, Health care issues, and 401k stuff.

Then there's Development, which is at the core of an Internet company. This area usually consists of all the network, MIS, and programming gurus. The servers are maintained in this section, as well as the site architecture. If you don't get hired as a web designer within a design division (which usually answers to Marketing, or Creative), then you will most certainly find yourself as a web designer or web developer within the Development division.

An Internet startup can operate with as little as 1 or 2 people, to about 20 people. When the Internet company gets ramped up, it can usually operate smoothly with 30 to 60 people. When the company has established itself a bit more, it will usually move from 60 to the high hundreds, depending on the business model, and how successful the company is.

4.4.3 What Does This Mean For My Future?

All I can say is what you've heard time and time again. "The Future is what you make of it."…If you truly wish to become successful in your field, then you need to learn the basics, fundamentals, and then get your hands dirty with the hard and complicated stuff as well. Don't be afraid to ask questions. There's not a Senior programmer out there in this world who hasn't goofed up on a project before. Don't think others must be above your mentality simply because they hold a better title than you do, especially when you should be cornering these senior mentors and milking them for all their knowledge! Of course you need to have just a touch of ambition, and faith that you will learn from others. Then have the confidence to apply what you learn!

Also remember that no question is too silly to ask, even if it means you have to ask where the on/off button is for the computer. Even the top experts have basic computer trouble. They are so well skilled and experienced in their central field, that things which might seem trivial and easy actually become difficult tasks indeed.

If you have free time, and know for a fact that you can get away with playing video games, force yourself instead to pick up a book and learn. Or experiment with scripting languages you might not be comfortable with yet. Get exposed to as many languages, programs, and operating systems as you can. At some point, you will find yourself right back in the interview process for another company, all over again. It will be to your advantage to have not only the newly added skills of previous on-the-job experience and training, but to have exposure and experience with such a variety of tools.

4.4.4 Being Part of Something BIG!!!!!!!

What a coincidence that this book should conclude on the fourth sub section of the fourth chapter! We've covered a lot of ground in this book. Although, if there was any one thing I could stress most of all, it would be this: GO 4 IT! Believe in yourself and your capabilities, and you will simply achieve it. Now, go out there and make it happen. Get rich, and don't forget to send off your gratuitous donation to my home address! In fact, If you'd like to send me any unsolicited comments or feedback, feel free to email me at *hotllama@netzero.net* or *hotllama@hotmail.com*. Operators are standing by, so don't delay!

If by chance, you happen to become a major CEO of a bustling large company after learning from my tutelage, please call me up and offer me a job as Vice President or something. Oh, and by the way, welcome to the Wonderful World of Web.

ABOUT THE AUTHOR

Aaron Wester was born in Orlando, Florida. Having spent his youth hacking video games, he's since become a leading figure in the Internet community.

He's worked for Disney, Earthlink, United States House of Representatives, Idealab!, and NetZero. He and his lovely wife have two children, two dogs and a Llama.

0-595-21591-2